ADVERTISING
and
COMMERCIAL
SPEECH

Readings From *Communications and the Law, 4*

Edited by
The Honorable Theodore R. Kupferman

Meckler
Westport • London

Citations to the original appearance of articles collected in this volume appear at the back of this book.

Library of Congress Cataloging-in-Publication Data

Advertising and commercial speech / edited by Theodore R. Kupferman.
    p. cm. -- (Readings from Communications and the law)
   ISBN 0-88736-510-8 (alk. paper) : $
   1. Advertising laws -- United States. 2. Freedom of speech --United
States.   I. Kupferman, Theodore R.   II. Series.
KF 1614 . A 75A38   1990
343.73 ' 082 -- dc20
[347 . 30382]   89-31995
                                                                CIP

British Library Cataloguing in Publication Data

 Advertising and commercial speech : readings from
 communications and the law.
 1. United States. Advertising. Law
 I. Kupferman, Theordore R.   II. Communications and the
 law
 347. 303 ' 82

 ISBN 0-88736-510-8

Meckler Corporation, 11 Ferry Lane West, Westport, CT 06880.
Meckler Ltd., Grosvenor Gardens House, Grosvenor Gardens,
  London SW1W 0BS, U.K.

Printed on acid free paper.
Printed and bound in the United States of America.

CONTENTS

PREFACE

The nine articles included herein are by no means the last word on this subject, but they go a long way to being a definitive discussion of the constitutional and legal aspects.

From the *Scharlott* article originally published in the summer of 1980, we see the evolution of the commercial speech doctrine, where the United States Supreme Court originally held that commercial advertising had no First Amendment protection, to granting full protection for advertising.

Just 8 years later, the *Trauth* and *Huffman* article considers the most recent case on commercial speech and the retrenchment on constitutional protection and its implications.

The *Hatry* and *Katz* article discusses the problem of competitive and comparative advertising with competitors disparaging each other, while the *Gallo* article considers Lanham Act aspects of competitive advertising.

The *Wilcox*, *Shea* and *Hovland* articles consider the First Amendment doctrine in relation to alcohol advertising and regulation, while the *Vestal* article considers tobacco in a similar context.

The *Spellman* article takes us a little further afield to consider another aspect of the First Amendment as a defense against a charge of negligent commercial use. Of course, this defense would also apply in defamation cases as to which reference is made to the companion compilation volume on Defamation in this series of readings from *Communications and the Law*.

BRADFORD W. SCHARLOTT

The First Amendment Protection of Advertising in the Mass Media

Mr. Scharlott received an M.A. degree from the School of Journalism, Indiana University (Bloomington) in 1978. He is currently a student in mass communication Ph.D. program at the University of Wisconsin (Madison). He has worked as a police-beat reporter and is now teaching courses in news writing and reporting.

I.   INTRODUCTION

In 1941, in the case of *Valentine* v. *Chrestensen,* the United States Supreme Court held that the First Amendment does not protect "purely commercial advertising."[1] In 1975, in *Virginia Pharmacy* v. *Virginia Consumer Council,* the Court recognized that society benefits substantially from the free flow of commercial information. Therefore, it discarded the "commercial speech doctrine" laid down in *Chrestensen* and

The author wishes to thank Professors Mary Ann Yodelis Smith and Gordon Baldwin, both of the University of Wisconsin (Madison), for their advice and encouragement of this research.

1. 316 U.S. 52.

held that all advertising is entitled to some First Amendment protection.[2]

Virginia Pharmacy and related decisions have had a profound effect on advertising. In the last six years, the Supreme Court has struck down complete prohibitions on the advertising of abortions,[3] prescription drug prices,[4] lawyers' fees,[5] and contraceptives.[6] Indeed, it now appears that government may not completely prohibit the advertising of any legal product or service.[7]

But the Court reasoned in *Virginia Pharmacy* that "commonsense differences" between advertising and noncommercial expression dictate that advertising should receive a lower level of First Amendment protection. Among other things, the Court said that advertising can be held to a higher standard of truthfulness than noncommercial speech, and that prior restraint might be an appropriate remedy for false or misleading advertising.[8]

Where do the mass media stand in regard to the Supreme Court's new views on advertising? Can a newspaper, for instance, be subjected to a prior restraint order if it carries a false advertisement? The Supreme Court did not address such questions in *Virginia Pharmacy*, nor has it in subsequent cases. But from the principles the Court has laid down, one can infer the degree to which the First Amendment protects advertising in the mass media.

This essay will assess the relationship between mass media advertising and the First Amendment: in Part II, the evolution of the commercial speech doctrine will be reviewed; in Part III, the *Virginia Pharmacy* decision will be examined; in Part IV, an inquiry will be made into the social interests the Supreme Court has sought to promote in affording greater protection to advertising; in Part V, the legal boundaries of advertising in the mass media will be delineated; and in Part VI, a summary and conclusions are provided.

2. 425 U.S. 748, 762. "Commercial speech doctrine" is the term the Supreme Court used to refer to the notion advanced in Chrestensen that commercial speech does not deserve First Amendment protection. Commercial speech refers to advertising and other forms of communication, such as door-to-door solicitations, intended to promote sales.
3. Bigelow v. Virginia, 421 U.S. 809 (1974).
4. Virginia Pharmacy v. Virginia Consumer Council, 425 U.S. 748 (1975).
5. Bates v. State Bar of Arizona, 433 U.S. 350 (1977). *See* Steuer, *Problems in Lawyer Advertising,* 1 COMM. AND THE LAW 2 (1979).
6. Carey v. Population Services, 431 U.S. 678 (1977).
7. E.g., a U.S. district court held that Virginia could not completely prohibit the advertising of doctors' fees. Health Systems Agency v. Virginia State Board of Medicine, 424 F. Supp. 267 (1976). The medical profession was the final one whose members were prohibited from advertising.
8. 425 U.S. at 771-72.

II. THE EVOLUTION OF THE COMMERCIAL SPEECH DOCTRINE

The Supreme Court first considered whether advertising should be protected by the First Amendment in *Valentine* v. *Chrestensen*. Chrestensen had been restrained from distributing, in New York City streets, handbills that advertised that he had a submarine on exhibit. The police told Chrestensen that the city's sanitary code prohibited advertising with handbills, but added that handbills bearing a political protest were permissible. Chrestensen then had a protest against the city printed on the back of the handbills, but the police still would not let him distribute them.[9]

The Supreme Court held that the sanitary code had not unconstitutionally abridged Chrestensen's freedom of speech, stating that "the Constitution imposes no [First Amendment] restraint on government as respects purely commercial advertising." The Court did not believe that the protest on the handbills should invoke the protection of the First Amendment, because "the affixing of the protest against official conduct . . . was with the intent, and for the purpose, of evading the prohibition of the ordinance."[10] In other words, the Court decided that Chrestensen's primary purpose in distributing the handbills was commercial and, therefore, deemed the handbills unworthy of First Amendment protection.

The Supreme Court used the primary purpose test in a number of cases following *Chrestensen*.[11] Probably the most significant was *New York Times* v. *Sullivan*. An Alabama court had found the *Times* guilty of libeling certain public officials by publishing an advertisement that allegedly injured their reputations. The Court held that the advertisement was entitled to First Amendment protection because it "communicated claimed abuses and sought financial support on behalf of a movement whose existence and objectives are matters of the highest public concern."[12]

---

9. 316 U.S. 52-53.
10. *Id.*, 53-54.
11. E.g., in Murdock v. Pennsylvania, 319 U.S. 105, the Supreme Court held that license fees for booksellers could not be applied to those who sold religious material. The Court reasoned that "the mere fact that the religious literature is 'sold' . . . rather than 'donated' does not transform evangelicalism into a commercial enterprise." *Id.*, 111. Also, cf. Breard v. Alexandria, 341 U.S. 622 (solicitors for national magazines can be prohibited from canvassing door to door) and Martin v. Struthers, 319 U.S. 141 (those selling religious literature cannot be prohibited from canvassing door to door).
12. 376 U.S. 254, 265-66.

The *Times* case was arguably no different in principle than *Chrestensen*. In both cases, the advertisers had a commercial goal, but also expressed grievances. The primary purpose test was deficient because it was an all-or-nothing proposition—either an advertisement received full First Amendment protection or it received none. Moreover, the test gave the court no good way to assess the competing interests in cases involving advertising. One commentator concluded that the test became "subjective and dependent on the whim of the court."[13]

The last Supreme Court decision that relied on the commercial speech distinction of *Chrestensen* was *Pittsburgh Press* v. *Pittsburgh Commission on Human Rights* (1973).[14] In that case, a 5-4 majority held that the *Press* could be restrained from placing help-wanted advertisements in columns designated by sex. The Court maintained that the placement of the advertisements was not entitled to the protection of the First Amendment because the advertisements themselves were "classic examples of commercial speech." The Court rejected the argument that the distinction between commercial and other kinds of speech should be dropped. Whether or not that argument would have any merit in other situations, the Court reasoned, it was unpersuasive here, where "the commercial activity itself is illegal and the restriction on advertising is incidental to a valid limitation on economic activity."[15]

The commercial speech doctrine received a severe blow in *Bigelow* v. *Virginia* (1974).[16] The Supreme Court held unconstitutional a Virginia statute the prohibited all advertising relating to abortions. The statute was challenged by a newspaper editor who had been prosecuted for publishing an advertisement that revealed that abortions could be obtained in New York. The Court rejected Virginia's argument that the *Chrestensen* ruling should support the statute, saying that *Chrestensen* "obviously does not support any sweeping proposition that advertising is unprotected *per se*." But rather than hold that all advertising is protected by the First Amendment, the Court likened the abortion advertisement here to the editorial advertisement in *New York Times* v. *Sullivan*. The Court said that the abortion advertisement "did more than simply propose a commercial transaction. It contained factual material of clear 'public interest'."[17] Thus, the Court left open the possibility that the commercial speech doctrine might retain some viability.

13. Lonnborg, "The First Amendment on the Classified Page: Commercial Speech and the 1973 Supreme Court," (Master's thesis, University of Wisconsin-Madison, 1974), p. 18.
14. 413 U.S. 376.
15. *Id.,* 385-89.
16. 421 U.S. 809.
17. *Id.,* 823.

III.   VIRGINIA PHARMACY v. VIRGINIA CONSUMER COUNCIL

The Supreme Court adjudicated *Virginia Pharmacy* the year after *Bigelow*. A Virginia resident, who had to take prescription drugs on a daily basis, and two nonprofit organizations had challenged a Virginia statute that forbade any advertising of prescription drug prices by pharmacists. A U.S. district court struck down the statute.[18] The Supreme Court, in an opinion written by Justice Harry A. Blackmun, upheld the district court ruling. The Supreme Court noted that the advertising in question here was not controversial and thus could not meet the public interest test used in *Bigelow*. Therefore, the Court finally rejected the commercial speech doctrine and expressly extended the First Amendment to all commercial speech.[19]

In its rationale for the decision, the Court noted that the free flow of price information can be of great benefit to both the individual consumer and to society. The consumer's interest "may be as keen, if not keener by far, than his interest in the day's most urgent political debate."[20] And concerning society's interest, the Court reasoned:

> So long as we preserve a predominantly free enterprise economy, the allocation of our resources in large measure will be made through numerous private economic decisions. It is a matter of public interest that those decisions, in the aggregate, be intelligent and well informed. To this end, the free flow of commercial information is indispensable . . . And if it is indispensable to the proper allocation of resources in a free enterprise system, it is also indispensable to the formation of intelligent opinions as to how that system ought to be regulated or altered.[21]

The state had argued that if advertising were allowed, pharmacists' standards might fall, since many pharmacists might be forced into price competition that would necessitate cutting corners. But the Court said that "high professional standards, to a substantial extent, are guaranteed by the close regulation to which pharmacists in Virginia are subject."[22] The state also argued that advertising might induce customers to shop at

18. Virginia Consumer Council v. Virginia Pharmacy Board, 376 F. Supp. 683.
19. 425 U.S. at 762.
20. *Id.,* 763.
21. *Id.,* 765.
22. *Id.,* 768.

different pharmacies, making it difficult for pharmacists to monitor their drug-taking practices. But the Court noted that "the State's protectiveness of its citizens rests in large measure on the advantages of their being kept in ignorance."[23] The Court reasoned that instead of taking such a "paternalistic approach," it is better

> to assume that this information is not in itself harmful, that people will perceive their own best interests if only they are well enough informed, and that the best means to that end is to open the channels of communication rather than to close them.[24]

In what seems like an afterthought because it appears in a footnote at the end of the opinion, the Court laid the foundation for a new framework of First Amendment interpretation.[25] Even though commercial speech serves valuable social interests, there are still "commonsense differences" between it and other sorts of speech—differences which "suggest that a different degree of protection is necessary to insure that the flow of truthful and legitimate information is unimpaired." One difference is that the truth of an advertisement "may be more easily verifiable by its disseminator than, let us say, news reporting or political commentary, in that ordinarily the advertiser seeks to disseminate information about a specific product or service that he himself provides and presumably knows more about than anyone else." Also, advertising may be more "durable" than other kinds of speech, since it is indispensable to making profits. The "greater objectivity and hardiness" of commercial speech may

> make it less necessary to tolerate inaccurate statements for fear of silencing the speaker . . . . They may also make it appropriate to require that a commercial message appear in such a form, or include such additional information, warnings, and disclaimers, as are necessary to prevent its being deceptive . . . . They may also make inapplicable the prohibition against prior restraint.

Thus, in effect, the Court held that commercial speech is entitled to only a second-class level of First Amendment protection.

It should be noted that advertising has always been granted some degree of constitutional protection. Before *Virginia Pharmacy*, it was

23. *Id.*, 769.
24. *Id.*, 770.
25. *Id.*, note 24, 771-72.

protected by the Due Process and Equal Protection clauses of the Fifth and Fourteenth Amendments, which cover all economic activity. But to meet the requirements of these clauses, a state merely had to advance a rational basis for a statute regulating advertising—that is, show that the regulation was reasonably related to a proper legislative purpose.[26] In practice, this standard of protection meant that the Supreme Court paid great deference to state regulation of advertising.[27] By contrast, the Supreme Court has usually required the government to show more than a rational basis when a First Amendment interest has been involved. For example, the Court has said that in the area of political speech, any form of prior restraint bears "a heavy presumption against its constitutional validity."[28]

The Supreme Court in *Virginia Pharmacy* created for advertising a middle ground between no First Amendment protection and full First Amendment protection. The Court did not delineate all the contours of this new area of protection. But it did say that states could still regulate false and misleading advertising, and could reasonably restrict the time, place, and manner in which advertising takes place. And the Court noted that in this case, it was unnecessary to deal with the "special problems" of broadcasting.[29]

IV. THE FIRST AMENDMENT AND ADVERTISING: AN INQUIRY INTO VALUES

The Supreme Court in *Virginia Pharmacy* did not say that it was relying on any particular theory of First Amendment interpretation.

26. E.g., *see* Nebbia v. New York, 291 U.S. 502 (1934), in which the Court upheld state regulation of the sale price of milk. The Court said: "So far as the requirement of due process is concerned, and in the absence of other constitutional restrictions, a state is free to adopt whatever economic policy may reasonably be deemed to promote public welfare, and to enforce that policy by legislation adapted to its purpose." *See* also Head v. New Mexico, 374 U.S. 424 (1963), in which the Court upheld a New Mexico statute forbidding the publication or broadcast of advertising by optometrists. A newspaper publisher and radio station owner challenged the law because they had been enjoined by a New Mexico court from accepting advertisements from an optometrist in Texas.
27. E.g., *see* Railway Express Agency v. New York, 336 U.S. 106 (1949), in which the Court upheld a statute prohibiting advertising on trucks unless the advertising related to one's own business. The statute was challenged on equal protection grounds as being arbitrary, but the Court, not finding any obvious reason for the law, simply speculated as to what the state's rationale might have been.
28. New York Times v. U.S., 403 U.S. 713, 714 (1971).
29. 425 U.S. 770-73. In its reference to broadcasters, the Court implied that since broadcasters are on a different constitutional footing than those in the print media, the elevated status of commercial speech might not change the status quo in broadcast regulation. *See, infra.* text accompanying notes 58 through 61.

However, certain theoretical underpinnings can be discerned. In order to assess how worthy commercial speech is of First Amendment protection, it is useful to examine them.

Actually, two separate theoretical strands can be seen in *Virginia Pharmacy*. The more established line might be called the Meiklejohn interpretation of the First Amendment. In brief, Alexander Meiklejohn held that the First Amendment was intended by the Founding Fathers to ensure that citizens would be able to voice their opinions on public issues. Such First Amendment protection, Meiklejohn believed, would facilitate public decision-making in a democracy. The emphasis of this interpretation is not on the private rights of citizens but on their collective responsibility to govern themselves well.[30]

The Meiklejohn theory is seen most clearly, not in the majority opinion in *Virginia Pharmacy,* but in the separate opinions. Justice Rehnquist, in the sole dissent, said the majority opinion would "elevate commercial intercourse between a seller hawking his wares and a buyer seeking to strike a bargain to the same place as has been previously reserved for the marketplace of ideas."[31] Whether Rehnquist specifically had Meiklejohn's interpretation in mind, he embraced a view similar to Meiklejohn's.

Justice Stewart concurred with the majority, but in his separate opinion he too apparently embraced the Meiklejohn theory. Stewart said advertising is "confined to the promotion of specific goods and services," whereas, "[I]deological expression, be it oral, literary, pictorial or theatrical, is integrally related to the exposition of thought—thought that may shape our concepts of the whole universe of man."[32] And in the only other separate opinion, Chief Justice Warren Burger explicitly agreed with Stewart's assessment.[33] Even though Stewart and Burger would not deny commercial speech all First Amendment protection, they imply that it does not promote ends as valuable to society as those promoted by ideological expression.

Meiklejohn's interpretation can be seen in the majority opinion, but even more prominent is what might be called the marketplace theory of the First Amendment.[34] The apparent goal of the First Amendment un-

---

30. Brennan, *The Supreme Court and the Meiklejohn Interpretation of the First Amendment,* 79 HARV. L. REV. 1 (1965). Brennan acknowledges the influence Meiklejohn has had on the Supreme Court. *See* also Meiklejohn, *The First Amendment is an Absolute,* SUP. CT. REV. 245 (1961).
31. 425 U.S. at 781.
32. *Id.,* 779-80.
33. *Id.,* 774.
34. Baker, *Commercial Speech: A Problem in the Theory of Freedom,* 62 IOWA L. REV. 1 (1976). Baker examines at length the relationship of economics and the First Amendment, and he rejects what he calls the "marketplace image of the

der this interpretation is to ensure that the greatest amount of truthful information—economic as well as ideological—reaches the greatest number of citizens.[35] The emphasis in this view appears to be just as much on the individual as on society. The consumer benefits by being able to purchase goods intelligently, and society benefits because resources are allocated efficiently. The majority opinion suggested that these economic goals might be just as worthy of First Amendment protection as the political goals of Meiklejohn's theory when it noted that the consumer's interest in economic information "may be keener by far" than his interest in political debate.[36] Still, the majority paid deference to the Meiklejohn view. After noting that the free flow of commercial information is "indispensable to the formation of intelligent opinions" about the regulation of the economy, the Court stated: "Therefore, *even if* the First Amendment were thought to be primarily an instrument to enlighten public decisionmaking in a democracy, we could not say that the free flow of commercial information does not serve that goal [emphasis added]."[37] In other words, the Court justified its decision in terms of Meiklejohn's views. But the Court did so equivocally by using a double-negative construction ("we could not say [it] does not serve"), which perhaps was meant to suggest that commercial speech does not serve democratic goals to the same degree that ideological expression does.

The degree to which commercial speech, in the abstract, is worthy of First Amendment protection depends on which theory is used. Under the Meiklejohn interpretation, commercial speech would appear clearly less worthy of protection than ideological expression. Under the marketplace theory, commercial speech seems practically as worthy. In a few commercial speech cases since *Virginia Pharmacy,* the Court has leaned more toward the Meiklejohn interpretation.[38] However, the Court has in

First Amendment." I have taken the liberty of coining the term "marketplace theory" in order to describe what assumptions underlay the majority opinion in Virginia Pharmacy.

35. *See, supra,* text accompanying note 21. In his dissent, Rehnquist said sardonically that "there is nothing in the United States Constitution that requires the Virginia Legislature to hew to the teachings of Adam Smith." 425 U.S. at 748.

36. In regard to this point, Rehnquist said in his dissent: "It is undoubtedly arguable that many people in the country regard the choice of shampoo just as important as who may be elected to local, state, or national office, but that does not automatically bring information about competing shampoos within the protection of the First Amendment." 425 U.S. at 787.

37. *Id.,* 765.

38. E.g., in Ohralik v. State Bar, 98 S. Ct. 1912 (1978), the Court said: "To require a parity of constitutional protection for commercial and noncommercial speech alike could invite dilution, simply by a leveling process, of the force of the Amendment's guarantee with respect to the latter kind of speech. Rather than subject the First Amendment to such a devitalization, we instead have afforded

other cases reaffirmed that society benefits substantially from the free flow of commercial information.[39] Thus, it seems that a majority of the Court believes that commercial speech is, in the abstract, *nearly* as socially valuable, and thus deserving of First Amendment protection, as noncommercial expression.

But regardless of how socially valuable commercial speech might be intrinsically, all the Supreme Court justices agree that it *needs* less First Amendment protection than noncommercial expression.[40] To determine the appropriate level of protection the Court in *Virginia Pharmacy* adopted a balancing approach, weighing the First Amendment interests in the free flow of prescription drug prices against the state's interest in regulating such advertising.[41] In other commercial speech cases, the Court explicitly stated that a balancing test should be used to determine whether First Amendment protection should be extended to a particular sort of commercial speech.[42]

The Supreme Court has employed this balancing procedure in a number of commercial speech cases since *Virginia Pharmacy*, and the balance has been struck several times in favor of extending First Amendment protection.[43] These cases suggest that states may no longer completely suppress the advertising of any legal product or service.[44]

commercial speech a limited measure of protection, commensurate with its subordinate position in the scale of First Amendment values, while allowing modes of regulation that might be impermissible in the realm of noncommercial speech." *See* also Young v. American Mini Theatres, 427 U.S. 50 (1976), where the Court relies on Stewart's concurring opinion in Virginia Pharmacy, in note 32.

39. E.g., in Linmark v. Willingboro, 431 U.S. 85 (1978), the Court struck down a ban on "For Sale" signs in front of houses, reasoning: "[T]he societal interest in 'the free flow of commercial information,' . . . is in no way lessened by the fact that the subject of the commercial information here is realty rather than abortions or drugs." And in First National Bank of Boston v. Bellotti, 435 U.S. 765 (1978), the Court said: [Our] recent commercial speech cases . . . illustrate that the First Amendment goes beyond protection of the press and the self-expression of individuals to prohibit government from limiting the stock of information from which members of the public may draw." *Id.,* 784. In this case, the Court held that a corporation could not be prohibited from issuing political advertisements.
40. *See supra,* text accompanying note 25.
41. 425 U.S. at 766-70.
42. In Bigelow, the Court said that simply because a state characterizes speech as commercial, it "may not completely escape the task of assessing the First Amendment interest at stake and weighing it against the public interest allegedly served by the regulation." 425 U.S. at 826. *See also* Pittsburgh Press, 413 U.S. at 389.
43. *See supra,* notes 3-7.
44. In Virginia Pharmacy, the Court said that, in regard to the advertising of drug prices, states may no longer "completely suppress the dissemination of concededly truthful information about entirely lawful activity." However, the Court at that time said it would reserve judgment about advertising by certain professionals. 425 U.S. at 773.

V.   THE LEGAL LIMITS OF ADVERTISING IN THE MASS MEDIA

Although complete bans on the advertising of legal products and services are no longer permissible, the Supreme Court said in *Virginia Pharmacy* that government may still deal with false or misleading advertising, may reasonably restrict the time, place, and manner in which advertising takes place, and may impose sanctions against illegal advertising.[45] It will be shown, however, that these various means of regulating advertising should be quite limited in regard to advertising that has entered the mass media. In other words, the mass media should be shielded by the First Amendment from most (but perhaps not all) forms of commercial speech regulation.

A.   False or Misleading Advertising

False or misleading advertising has long been regulated by government. At the federal level, the Federal Trade Commission is empowered to ensure the truthfulness of advertising.[46] And virtually all of the states have regulated false advertising since early in this century.[47] In *Virginia Pharmacy,* the Supreme Court said: "Untruthful speech, commercial or otherwise, has never been protected for its own sake. . . . We foresee no obstacle to a State's dealing effectively with [false or misleading advertising]."[48]

As noted, the Supreme Court said government could remedy misleading advertising by requiring that advertisements include certain sorts of information, and it added that prior restraints might be appropriate. The Court reasoned that such remedies would be permissible because advertising is easily verifiable and because it is resistant to being chilled by regulation, since it is important to making profits.[49] It is important to note that those characteristics of advertising are true only as they relate to advertisers themselves. The mass media are in no better position to

---

45. *Id.,* 770-73.
46. Federal Trade Commission Act 12, 15 U.S.C. §52 (1976). *See* Johnson, *The Federal Trade Commission: An Evolution in Social Engineering,* 1 COMM. AND THE LAW 3 (1979).
47. For an overview, *see* NELSON and TEETER, LAW OF MASS COMMUNICATIONS (1973), 550-52. Also, in an apparent attempt to limit the scope of Virginia Pharmacy, the Supreme Court held in Friedman v. Rogers, 59 LE2d 100 (1979) that the state of Texas could constitutionally ban the practice of optometry under a trade name, reasoning that the use of trade names could lead to deceptive or misleading advertising.
48. 425 U.S. at 771.
49. *See supra,* text accompanying note 25.

ascertain the accuracy of the advertisements they carry than they are to ascertain the accuracy of their news stories—and, indeed, they have much less incentive to make sure advertisements are factually correct, since their ultimate success depends far more on the accuracy of their news. Likewise, the media cannot ensure the durability of advertising; their total revenue depends on a great number of advertisements, and therefore their total interest in any particular advertisement or kind of advertising is slight.[50]

Since the mass media are in a poor position to ensure either the accuracy or the durability of advertising, it follows that government should not try to eliminate false or misleading advertising by way of regulating the media. To do so could have a chilling effect on the flow of commercial information to society. For example, to threaten a newspaper with prior restraint could inhibit the paper from accepting advertisements from unfamiliar advertisers, especially if a restraining order could involve holding back copies already printed.[51] Moreover, for the government to insist that the mass media somehow screen advertisements for falsity or other evils would smack of the paternalistic approach to consumers' welfare deprecated in *Virginia Pharmacy*.[52] If an advertisement seems suspect on its face, then consumers should be assumed capable of evaluating it. Logically, then, government should have no greater interest in regulating the truthfulness of advertising in the mass media than it does in regulating the truthfulness of ideological expression in the mass media.

B. Time, Place, and Manner Restrictions

The Supreme Court specified in *Virginia Pharmacy* that government could restrict the time, place, and manner in which advertising

---

50. These observations on the relationship between advertising and the mass media are made in Merrill, *First Amendment Protection for Commercial Advertising: The New Constitutional Doctrine*, 44 U NIV. OF C HI. L. REV. 205, 251-53 (1977).
51. There is legal precedent for not subjecting publications to prior restraint because they contain false advertisements. In Goldsmith v. Jewish Press Pub. Co., 118 Misc. 789, 195 N.Y. Supp. 37 (1922), the court held that a newspaper could not be enjoined from publishing a false advertisement, since the editor had no knowledge of its falsity. See 89 A.L.R. 1004-1007.
52. Concerning product liability, a New Jersey appellate court held that Popular Mechanics magazine was not liable for injuries caused by firecrackers advertised in the magazine. The court said that to hold magazines, newspapers and other publications liable for products they advertise but do not endorse would "not only be impractical and unrealistic, but would have a staggering adverse effect on the commercial world and our economic system." Yuhas v. Mudge 322 A.2d 824, 825 (1974).

takes place, as long as such restrictions "are justified without reference to the content of the regulated speech, that they serve a significant governmental interest, and that in doing so they leave open ample alternative channels for communication of the information."[53] Time, place, and manner restrictions have been justified as exercises of the states' police power to prevent public nuisances (e.g., loud speakers),[54] to reduce traffic problems (e.g., advertising vehicles),[55] and to preserve aesthetic values (e.g., billboards).[56]

Time, place, and manner restrictions probably cannot affect advertising as it appears in the print media, partly because of the nature of these media. A publication is bound to neither a specific time nor place, and thus it can be affected by such restrictions only insofar as it represents a "manner"—that is, print—of communication. However, a statute prohibiting some form of advertising from being printed in publications would be extremely restrictive; thus, it probably could not meet the requirement that "ample alternative channels for communication" be left open. Indeed, in *Bigelow* v. *Virginia,* the Supreme Court strongly suggested that the print media enjoy a special constitutional status in commercial speech cases:

> The strength of [Bigelow's] interest was augmented by the fact that the statute was applied against him as a publisher and editor of a newspaper, not against the advertiser or a referral agency or a practitioner. The prosecution thus incurred more serious First Amendment overtones.[57]

The broadcast media, however, are susceptible to time, place, and manner restrictions. For one thing, broadcasts are bound to specific times and places. For another, broadcast signals are so pervasive that without regulation some people (or their children) could be inadvertently subjected to communications they consider offensive. And finally, since the airwaves are considered public property, broadcasters (unlike publishers) can be required to act in the public interest. For these reasons, it has long been established that broadcasting receives less First Amendment protection than the print media.[58] Thus, Congress was able to prohibit cigarette advertising over the airwaves.[59] And the Federal

---

53. 425 U.S., at 771.
54. Kovacs v. Cooper, 336 U.S. 77 (1949).
55. Fifth Ave. Coach Co. v. New York, 221 U.S. 476 (1911).
56. Mojeska Sign Studios, Inc. v. Berle, 390 N.Y.S.2d 945 (St. Ct. 1977).
57. 421 U.S., at 828-29.
58. *See* National Broadcasting Co. v. U.S., 319 U.S. 190 (1943), 226-27.
59. 28 U.S.C. §§2282 and 2284. Upheld in Capital Broadcasting v. Mitchell, 333 F. Supp. 582 (1971).

Communications Commission has been found to have the authority to prohibit language it deems offensive, or to restrict the hours in which such language may be aired.[60] As noted, the Supreme Court in *Virginia Pharmacy* explicitly set aside any consideration of whether the elevated standing of commercial speech would affect broadcasters.[61]

C.   Regulation of Illegal Advertising

In at least one area, government may enjoy extra latitude in regulating commercial speech in the mass media. The case of *Pittsburgh Press* set forth the principle that advertising that encourages illegal activity may be proscribed.[62] The principle itself may well be defensible, but the important question is: What constitutes such impermissible advertising? In the area of noncommercial speech, expression advocating criminal activity can be punished only if it is both *intended* to incite criminal activity and *likely* to do so.[63] In the *Press* case, the court apparently applied a less stringent standard. As noted, the *Press* was found guilty of encouraging sex discrimination in hiring practices because it placed help-wanted advertisements under columns designated by sex. But the paper's editors apparently did not intend to incite lawless activity; before each column they placed a notice stating that the sex-designated headings were meant only for convenience and not for discriminatory purposes.[64]

Pittsburgh Press was adjudicated before the demise of the commercial speech doctrine, and the Court relied on *Chrestensen* to preclude extending First Amendment protection to the paper.[65] The case might have had a different outcome if decided after *Virginia Pharmacy*. However, it was cited in *Virginia Pharmacy* as a valid limitation on media advertising.[66] Thus, if a state can characterize a type of advertising as being conducive of illegal activity, the state may be allowed to regulate or suppress it.

The Supreme Court, however, will probably no longer be as deferen-

---

60. *See* F.C.C. v. Pacifica Foundation, 98 S.Ct. 3026 (1978), in which the Court upheld the right of the FCC to restrict the hours during which a George Carlin monologue could be played. *See* Tickton, *Obscene/Indecent Programming: The FCC and WBAI*, 1 COMM. AND THE LAW 3 (1979).
61. 425 U.S. at 773.
62. 412 U.S. 376.
63. Brandenburg v. Ohio, 395 U.S. 444.
64. 413 U.S. at 394.
65. *Id.*, 387-88.
66. 425 U.S. at 772.

tial as it was in *Pittsburgh Press* to a state's finding that a certain type of advertising encourages illegal activity. In *Carey* v. *Population Services International,* New York tried to justify a total ban on contraceptive advertising on the premise that such advertising encourages illicit sexual activity among young people. The Court struck down the advertising ban, saying that "none of the advertisements in this record can even remotely be characterized as '*directed to inciting* or producing imminent lawless action and . . . *likely to incite* or produce such action.' *Brandenburg* v. *Ohio* . . . [emphasis added]."[67] In other words, the Court used the stringent standard of non-commercial speech to determine if contraceptive advertisements conduced illegal activity. The test of illegality used in *Carey* should afford greater protection to advertising—and by extension to the mass media that carry it—than did the test used in *Pittsburgh Press.*

It should be noted that advertising is subject to the same limitations as noncommercial speech. Thus, a state may find a person guilty of violating obscenity laws for pandering to prurient interests in an advertisement.[68] Also, advertisements that damage reputations may be the basis for libel convictions.[69]

VI. SUMMARY AND CONCLUSIONS

When the Supreme Court brought all advertising within the protection of the First Amendment in *Virginia Pharmacy,* it opened unexplored territory. Since then, the Court has in a number of cases delineated in part the First Amendment rights of advertising. These cases make it apparent that government cannot completely suppress the advertising of any particular product or service. Nonetheless, false and misleading advertising can be regulated, as can advertising that conduces illegal activity. And the circumstances under which advertising can take place may be restricted.

The Supreme Court's greater solicitude for advertising seems based

---

67. 431 U.S. 678, 700.
68. *See,* e.g., Splawn v. California, 431 U.S. 595 (1977), where the Court upheld an obscenity conviction that was based on the content of an advertisement. Significantly, a dissent by Justice Stevens, joined by three other justices, would have reversed the conviction in light of Virginia Pharmacy because the advertisement was truthful and made for a commercial purpose.
69. In Peck v. Tribune, 214 U.S. 185 (1909), Justice Holmes held for the Court that a newspaper could be found guilty of libel for printing the picture of a teetotaler over an endorsement in a whiskey advertisement. For general guidelines in libel cases, see Gertz v. Welch, 418 U.S. 323 (1974).

in part on a new kind of First Amendment interpretation which emphasizes the commercial needs of both individuals and society. However, this new interpretation is partly at odds with the more established view that the First Amendment was intended primarily to promote public decision making in a democracy. The Court's recent decisions indicate that it deems advertising nearly as worthy of First Amendment protection as ideological speech. But the Court has said that advertising needs less First Amendment protection because advertisers are familiar with their own products and have a financial stake in advertising that makes it resistant to being chilled by regulation.

No Supreme Court cases since *Virginia Pharmacy* have dealt with advertising in the mass media. Thus, publishers and broadcasters have no clear guide as to how much First Amendment protection they should receive for the advertising they carry. However, the principles the Supreme Court has laid down suggest that advertising in the mass media should receive more First Amendment protection than advertisers themselves receive. One reason for this is that those in the mass media are in a poor position to ensure either the accuracy or the durability of advertising. Another reason is that the mass media play a crucial role in disseminating advertising broadly.

Thus, government should not be able to regulate advertising in the mass media to a much greater extent than it can regulate ideological speech in the mass media—at least so far as the print media are concerned. The Supreme Court has suggested that the "special problems" of broadcasting may make the new First Amendment protection for advertising inapplicable to the broadcast media.

Although the Supreme Court has not explicitly said so, the Court would probably differentiate between the First Amendment protection given advertising at its source—the advertisers themselves—and the protection given advertising once it appears in the mass media. Government, it seems, should properly try to regulate advertising at the source.

PATRICIA HATRY
JEFFREY C. KATZ

Comparative Advertising Law and a Recent Case Thereon

Patricia Hatry is a partner and Jeffrey
C. Katz an associate in the law firm of
Davis & Gilbert

THE TIC TAC CASE

> "I've got a confession to make. I've always loved the
> freshness of Tic Tac. But when sugar-frees came
> along, I figured I'd give up some of that freshness to
> get fewer calories. Know what? I was wrong. Sugar
> Free Velamints have 9 calories and Tic Tac has 1-1/2.
> Not 9. 1-1/2. So I'm staying with Tic Tac. Because, to
> get fewer calories you don't have to give up taste, or
> freshness or nothin'. Tic Tac. The 1-1/2 calorie mint."

This familiar commercial[1] spawned one of the most interesting
comparative advertising cases to date, Ragold, Inc. v. Ferrero, U.S.A.
Inc. and Altschiller, Reitzfeld, Jackson & Solin, Inc.[2] The crux of the

1. 30-second and 10-second versions of the commercial were involved in addition to trade promotional material.
2. 506 F. Supp, 117 (N.D. Ill. 1980).

litigation was Ragold's claim that a comparison of the caloric content of two candy mints of unequal size[3] was deceptive to consumers and unfairly disparaged Velamints.

Ragold proceeded by application for a temporary restraining order to enjoin defendants' television commercials and trade advertising under Section 43(a) of the Lanham Act.[4] The application was heard promptly by Judge Marvin E. Aspen who in his comprehensive opinion outlined the "well established" elements of a claim for deceptive comparative advertising. A plaintiff must show "(1) the defendant has made false statements of fact as to its own product, with such falsity stemming from actual misstatements, partially correct statements, or failures to disclose; (2) there is actual deception or at least a tendency to deceive a substantial section of the audience; (3) the deception must be material, in that it is likely to influence purchasing decisions; (4) the advertised goods traveled in interstate commerce; and (5) there is likelihood of injury, stemming either from a decline in sales or loss in good will."

Plaintiff's position was set forth by Judge Aspen as follows: "The essential premise underlying plaintiff's claim that the commercial misrepresents the respective calorie content of Tic Tac and Velamints is that the appropriate unit of comparison is by weight rather than by individual mint. From this premise flows plaintiff's other two contentions: that the advertisement fails to reflect adequately the respective sizes of Tic Tac and Velamints, and neglects to inform viewers that the promise of fewer calories depends on the consumption of fewer than six Tic Tacs for every Velamint."

Since the Tic Tac advertisements were attacked on the basis that they were deceptive due to the nature of the presentation rather than because of any literal falsehood, the Court's role was limited to determining the reaction of the group to which the advertisement was directed, for, as frequently quoted, his own subjective reaction would be "at best not determinative and at worst irrelevant."[5]

Plaintiff relied on a consumer survey and a pair of Federal Trade Commission decisions[6] to support its proposition that comparisons of

3. Ragold's Velamints is approximately six times the size of Ferrero's Tic Tac.
4. 15 U.S.C. § 1125(a).
5. 506 F. Supp. at 125, quoting *American Home Products Corp.* v. *Johnson & Johnson*, 577 F.2d 160, 165-166 (2d Cir. 1978); *McNeilab, Inc.* v. *American Home Products Corp.*, 207 USPQ 573, 579 (S.D.N.Y. 1980); *American Brands, Inc.* v. *R.J. Reynolds*, 413 F. Supp. 1352, 1357 (S.D.N.Y. 1976).
6. *In the Matter of National Bakers Services, Inc.*, 62 FTC 1115 (1963), *aff'd sub nom, National Bakers Services, Inc.* v. *F.T.C.*, 329 F.2d 365 (7th Cir. 1964) and *In the Matter of Bakers Franchise Corp.*, 59 FTC 70 (1961), *aff'd sub nom, Bakers Franchise Corp.,* v. *F.T.C.*, 302 F.2d 258 (3d Cir. 1962).

products of non-equivalent weight are inherently misleading and that caloric content by weight is the appropriate basis for comparing Tic Tac and Velamints. The consumer survey was discussed primarily in a foot-note reference which noted the small sample size—only 30 persons—and sketchy findings. The FTC cases cited involved the claim that the advertised breads were lower in calorie content having been achieved by packaging one-pound loaves of bread in 18 gram slices instead of the standard 23 gram slice. Since Tic Tac is a lower calorie product when measured either on a per mint or per package basis, Judge Aspen did not find the FTC decisions persuasive and concluded:

> "Since plaintiff has failed to show that mint or package size are inappropriate units of comparison, the consumer impression cannot at this point be said to support a conclusion that plaintiff has shown a likelihood of prevailing on its claim that the advertisement carries a false calorie message which has a tendency to deceive the consumer audience."

The Court's position on whether the television commercials should affirmatively disclose that six Tic Tac mints have the same caloric content as one Velamint and should show the relative dimensions of the two mints was set forth as follows:

> "The commercial, both through graphics and the written word, clearly indicates to consumers that each Tic Tac contains roughly one-sixth the calories in a single Velamint. In the Court's judgment, it is not unreasonable to expect that the viewing audience will be able to make the calculation that Tic Tac will not be less caloric if consumed in more than a six-to-one ratio than they would consume Velamints. Similarly, the Court rejects plaintiff's contention that the visual comparison of Tic Tac and Velamints is insufficient because it is unidimensional and fails to convey adequately the relative size of the two mints. The inability of the television medium to convey in full the dimensional properties of objects no doubt presents certain difficulties in comparative advertising situations. However, it is the Court's view that the visual comparison provided in the commercial is sufficient to apprise consumers of the different sizes of the respective mints. This is so particularly since the graphic is accompanied by the respective calorie content per

mint, thus providing further information from which the consumer might infer that the size of Tic Tac is roughly one-sixth that of Velamints, the same as the calorie proportion of Tic Tac to Velamints. Moreover, taken to its logical end, plaintiff's argument would lead to the result that all visual comparisons of products of disparate size are inaccurate and thus misleading. The Court is unwilling to endorse such a rule."

Plaintiff's application for a temporary restraining order was denied and an expedited discovery and briefing schedule for a preliminary injunction hearing was ordered.[7] Defendant filed application for a preliminary injunction on its counterclaims that plaintiff's labeling and advertising misrepresented the caloric content of Velamints to consumers who were led to believe that Velamints had few or no calories. The ensuing discovery period extended well beyond the projected schedule, including numerous interrogatories, depositions and document productions rivaling pretrial procedures in antitrust litigations (the competing mint manufacturers had even prior to litigation amassed a virtual compendium of marketing studies). After rounds of negotiations and hundreds of telephone communications, the case was settled, leaving Judge Aspen's decision and a "minty" case for moot court argument and law school discourse.

GENESIS OF THE LAW

It is generally accepted that the current genre of comparative advertising, i.e., that of naming the competitors, had its beginnings in the early 1960's with the Doyle Dane Bernbach advertising campaign for Avis—"We Try Harder." While Hertz was not directly named in the Avis advertisements, the reference to "Number One" made the target clear. Previously, comparative advertising typically employed references to Brand X as the object of the comparison. Naming competitors was regarded as unethical and bad for business. In addition, the three major television networks did not at that time accept directly comparative advertisements.

The success of the Avis campaign encouraged other advertisers to pursue comparative advertising campaigns and perhaps provided the impetus for the change in industry attitude. In 1971 NBC announced that it would begin accepting comparative advertisements. In 1972 the

7. Both parties had declined the offer of the court to convert the TRO proceeding into a preliminary injunction hearing.

staff of the Federal Trade Commission prodded CBS and ABC into discontinuing their blanket bans on comparative advertising.[8] The American Association of Advertising Agencies (the 4A's) issued its "Policy Statement and Guidelines for Comparative Advertising"; the National Association of Broadcasters (NAB) Code Authority issued its "Comparative Advertising Guidelines" in 1975; the National Advertising Review Board issued its guidelines, "Identifying Competitors in Advertising", in 1977.

In 1979 the Federal Trade Commission published its policy statement on comparative advertising wherein it stated:

> "Commission policy in the area of comparative advertising encourages the naming of, or reference to competitors, but requires clarity, and, if necessary, disclosure to avoid deception of the consumer. Additionally, the use of truthful comparative advertising should not be restrained by broadcasters or self-regulation entities."[9]

The FTC further stated:

> "Comparative advertising, when truthful and nondeceptive, is a source of important information to consumers and assists them in making rational purchase decisions. Comparative advertising encourages product improvement and innovation, and can lead to lower prices in the marketplace. For these reasons, the Commission will continue to scrutinize carefully restraints upon its use.[10]

During recent years comparative advertising has proliferated. Nevertheless, there are few litigated cases in this area, due in part to the caution exercised by the networks in accepting comparative advertising and the advertising industry's voluntary system of self-regulation.[11]

---

8. Sterk, The Law of Comparative Advertising: How Much Worse is "Better" than "Great", 67 TMR 368, 369-70 (1977).
9. 44 Fed.Reg. 47328, August 13, 1979.
10. *Id.* at 47329.
11. Complaints about advertising may be filed with the Council's National Advertising Division (NAD), with an appeal to the National Advertising Review Board (NARB).

Section 43(a) of the Lanham Act,[12] which for the first few decades of its existence was rarely employed to protect against advertising abuses,[13] has become the primary weapon for complainants in comparative advertising cases.

Many of the 43(a) cases involved advertisements for cheap copies of more expensive products, implying parity at a cheaper price rather than superiority. Where the defendant has disclosed that its product is a copy, the courts have been reluctant to find a violation,[14] but where defendant uses a picture of plaintiff's product in its advertising and impliedly misrepresents this as his own product, the courts are inclined to recognize a cause of action under Section 43(a).[15]

Although the forerunner cases did not involve comparative advertisements as such, they expanded the ambit of 43(a), thus providing the foundation for application of the section to redress claims for false comparative advertising.

A FEW LANDMARK CASES

In *Smith* v. *Chanel, Inc.*[16] plaintiff advertised its fragrance "Second Chance" as a duplicate of defendant's "Chanel No. 5" at a fraction of

12. Section 43(a), 15 U.S.C. § 1125(a) (1946), provides:
   Any person who shall affix, apply or annex, or use in connection with any goods or services, or any container or containers for goods, a false designation of origin, or any false description or representation, including words or other symbols tending falsely to describe or represent the same, and shall cause such goods or services to enter into commerce, and any person who shall with knowledge of the falsity of such designation of origin or description or representation cause or procure the same to be transported or used in commerce or deliver the same to any carrier to be transported or used, shall be liable to civil action by any person doing business in the locality falsely indicated as that of origin or in the region in which said locality is situated, or by any person who believes that he is or is likely to be damaged by the use of any such false description or representation.
13. It has been observed that from 1946 to 1964, a total of fewer than thirty reported cases had arisen, under Section 43(a), not all of which even dealt with advertising situations. Sterk, *supra*, note 8, at 381 n. 63.
14. See *Societe Comptoir de l'Industrie Cotonniere, Etablissements Boussac* v. *Alexander's Department Stores*, 299 F.2d 33 (2d Cir. 1962) (No violation where defendant advertised its garments "Original by Christian Dior—Alexander's Exclusive-Paris-Adaptation"); *George O'Day Associates, Inc.* v. *Talman Corp.*, 206 F.Supp. 297 (D.R.I. 1962), *aff'd* 310 F.2d 623 (1st Cir. 1962) (No violation where defendant's picture of its sailboat was not an exact duplicate of plaintiff's boat).
15. See *Zandelin* v. *Maxwell Bentley Mfg. Co., Inc.*, 197 F.Supp. 608 (S.D.N.Y. 1961); *General Pool Corp.* v. *Hallmark Pool Corp.*, 259 F.Supp. 383 (N.D. Ill. 1966).
16. 402 F.2d 562 (9th Cir. 1968).

the price. The trial court granted a preliminary injunction on the basis that defendant had appropriated plaintiff's good will and, regardless of the truth or falsity of the claims, there was trademark infringement. The Ninth Circuit reversed, holding that the copier of an unpatented product may use its trademark in his advertising to identify the product he has copied so long as the advertising does not contain misrepresentations or create a reasonable likelihood of confusion as to the source of the product. The Ninth Circuit was of the view that protection of trademark values should be limited to source identification, on the basis that extension of protection to the trademark's good will would have serious anti-competitive consequences and that this public policy consideration outweighed the involved trademark interests.

On remand, the District Court[17] circumvented the holding of the appeal court and found again for plaintiff. Relying on the results of a chemical test, the court noted that the composition of "Second Chance" was in fact not identical to that of "Chanel No. 5", hence the perfumes could not smell the same, and a permanent injunction was warranted.

Bernard Food Industries, Inc. v. *Dietene.*[18] In 1964, Bernard began manufacturing an eggless custard product. In 1965, Dietene and Bernard both started marketing an egg custard product. In 1966 Dietene's chemist, without knowledge of Bernard's egg custard product, made a comparison of Dietene's egg custard with Bernard's eggless custard and found Dietene's product superior. That comparison sheet was distributed to Dietene employees and salesmen, not to customers or potential customers. The District Court found that Dietene misrepresented its own product to plaintiff's detriment. The Court of Appeals found no evidence that the analysis of the specified products was false and reversed on the basis that any misrepresentations related to Bernard's product, not to that manufactured by Dietene.

While the decision has been criticized[19] as drawing an unnecessary distinction between misrepresenting one's own product and that of a competitor, its holding that false representations by a defendant about a plaintiff's product are not covered by Section 43(a) has been regularly paid homage in successive judicial opinions.

In recent years, two industries have accounted for more than their fair share of Section 43(a) comparative advertising cases — the cigarette and pharmaceutical industries — and the Southern District of New York

---

17. 178 USPQ 630 (N.D. Cal. 1973). The case was once again appealed, and grant of injunction affirmed, 528 F.2d 284 (9th Cir. 1976).
18. 415 F.2d 1279 (7th Cir. 1969). One commentator has labeled this case as "perhaps the most significant comparative advertising case which has arisen under Section 43(a)." Sterk, *supra,* note 8, at 382.
19. *Skil Corp.* v. *Rockwell International Corp.,* 375 F.Supp. 777, 782 n. 10 (N.D. Ill. 1974).

has been the forum for their judicial resolution.

American Brands, Inc. v. *R.J. Reynolds Tobacco Co.*[20] involves superlative rather than strictly comparative claims. Reynolds advertised its Now 2 mg. tar cigarettes as "Now. The lowest 'tar' of all cigarettes." American Brands claimed the advertising was false, primarily because American manufactured a 1 mg. tar cigarette, Carlton 70's, which was lower in tar and nicotine content than Now. During the course of the litigation, Reynolds modified this claim to: "Now - 2 mg. 'tar' is lowest (king-size or longer)".

Reynolds filed counterclaims alleging that American's advertising was misleading on a number of grounds, including its claim that Carlton 2 is the "fastest growing of the top 25" brands and its listing of other cigarettes' tar content which omitted Now, thereby implying, Reynolds claimed, that no other cigarette was as low in tar as Carlton 2's.

Since no evidence of consumer reaction was introduced to show that the claim ["Now - 2 mg. 'tar' is lowest (King size or longer)"] creates the impression that there is no cigarette lower in tar, Judge Lasker held that American failed to prove tendency to deceive. Similarly the various counterclaims were dismissed for failure of proof. The relief granted on the preliminary injunction, which was merged into a full trial under Rule 65 of the Federal Rules of Civil Procedure, was limited to judicial direction that billboard and promotional material still containing the discontinued "lowest tar" claim be removed from the marketplace.

Philip Morris Incorporated v. *Loew's Theatres, Inc. d/b/a Lorillard.*[21] In April 1980 SE Surveys, Inc., commissioned by Lorillard, conducted what was labeled "A National Taste Test: Triumph Menthol vs Winston Lights, Marlboro Lights, Vantage and Merit Non-Menthols". Numerical superiority on the basis of taste was not established, the test name was held literally false, and preliminary injunctive relief was granted.

Additionally, Philip Morris submitted a survey which showed that 37% of those interviewed (the largest block of those answering the open-ended question) believed that the advertisement in which the survey was cited claimed that Triumph tastes better than Merit. Despite Lorillard's counter of expert testimony to attack the methodology of the survey, other expert testimony to justify its advertising, and proof of identical advertising practices which resulted in its larger market share, Judge Sweet held:

> "The misleading implication resulting from the use of
> the percentages favoring Triumph and the omission of

20. 413 F.Supp. 1352 (S.D.N.Y. 1976).
21. 80 Civ. 4082 (S.D.N.Y. July 26, 1980), not reported.

the similar percentage for Merit is demonstrated by the results of the survey of consumer reaction to the Lorillard ad submitted by plaintiff. Though the statement is statistically accurate, the omission of the percentages established by the Test with their clear implication with respect to taste has caused the ads to be deceptive to the general public as established by Philip Morris's weekend survey, despite its acceptability to those experienced in advertising."[22]

Judge Sweet in his opinion underscored the need for injunctive relief since money damages are not available under current court standards:

"No measure of the competition for the mind of the consumer has yet been devised other than market share, and no evidence has been, or probably could ever be submitted, that would establish that a particular market share shift was a direct result of a false advertisement so that money damages could be determined. Brand loyalty would be affected and by its very nature would remain incalculable."[23]

In the related 1980 case, *R.J. Reynolds Tobacco Company* v. *Loew's Theatres, Inc. d.b.a. Lorillard and/or Lorillard U.S.A.,*[24] decided three months later, Lorillard modified its advertising to claim "Triumph beats [Winston Lights]" and "Triumph at less than [one-fourth] the tar, preferred over [Winston Lights]." The test, for advertising purpose, was renamed "National Smoker Study Winner". No less than eleven consumer surveys were presented to the court in addition to the challenged Lorillard Smoker Study.

Judge Sweet in his thoughtful opinion noted that no court had previously "enjoined comparative advertising because of the consumer survey methodology underlying the ad."; that although the test was not of the quality necessary to support an advertising campaign, rather was of the "quick and dirty" variety, nevertheless it had been conducted and the ads based on the mall intercept study were not literally false. However, plaintiff's tests replicating those of defendant, with different results obtaining, demonstrated built-in bias (through disclosure of tar content just before participants were asked which cigarette they would prefer to smoke, thus eliciting "tar preference" as distinguished from

22. *Id.,* slip op. at 7.
23. *Id.,* slip op. at 8.
24. 80 Civ. 4197 (S.D.N.Y. October 24, 1980), not reported.

the advertised "overall preference"). Consumer perception studies showed further that "somewhere between one-fifth to one-third of those surveyed carry away from the ad the report of a Triumph *taste victory.*"[25] Consequently, a preliminary order was entered *pendente lite* against further use of the phrase "overall preference" or any substantial equivalent including any specific reference to taste or national percentages.

American Home Products Corp. v. *Johnson & Johnson*[26] concerned two Anacin advertisements: 1) a television commercial which said that Adult Strength Anacin for pain, other than headache pain, reduces the inflammation that often comes with pain, while Datril, Tylenol and Extra-Strength Tylenol (the latter two manufactured by McNeil Laboratories, Inc., a subsidiary of Johnson & Johnson) do not; the commercial then went on to specify inflammation of tooth extraction, muscle strain, backache, tendonitis and neuritis; and 2) a print advertisement headlined "Anacin Can Reduce Inflammation That Comes With Most Pain, Tylenol Cannot." McNeil complained to the three television networks and to the NAD (with respect to the print advertisement). Only ABC required a modification to the commercial; nevertheless, American Home decided to seek a declaratory judgment that the commercial did not violate the Lanham Act. McNeil seized the opportunity, pleaded conterclaims and moved for preliminary injunction.

Judge Stewart carefully reviewed the voluminous evidence introduced by both sides, which included, in addition to medical studies, articles and expert opinion, a Gallup & Robinson day-after-viewing telephone interview test of 61 television viewers who claimed to have seen and remembered the commercial and an ASI (Audience Studies, Inc.) special screening for 250 people of varying ages, income levels and occupations. Although two expert witnesses testified as to the meaning of the advertising, Judge Stewart placed more reliance on his own analysis of the consumer tests, including the verbatim consumer responses. Judge Stewart's opinion provides an excellent summary of the advantages and disadvantages of different methods of consumer testing—a veritable gold mine for potential cross-examination.

On appeal, the Second Circuit held that the District Court's use of consumer response data was proper, that since the advertising claims were deliberately ambiguous, "Judge Stewart was warranted in examining, and may have been compelled to examine, consumer data to determine first the messages conveyed in order to determine alternately the truth or falsity of the messages."[27] The Circuit Court affirmed Judge

25. *Id.*, slip op. at 18.
26. 436 F.Supp. 785 (S.D.N.Y. 1977), *aff'd* 577 F.2d 160 (2d Cir. 1978).
27. 577 F.2d at 166

Stewart's determinations that the advertising claimed greater pain relief and that aspirin and acetominophen (APAP) are equipotent as pain relievers for inflammatory conditions and held "it was perfectly proper for the trial court to enjoin future advertisements containing superior analgesic claims."[28]

McNeilab, Inc. v. *American Home Products Corporation.*[29] In 1979 American Home inaugurated a campaign for Maximum Strength Anacin (MSA), with two television commercials containing superlative as distinguished from directly comparative claims. The advertising claimed that MSA "contains more of the pain reliever doctors recommend most. More than regular strength. Maximum Strength. The Maximum Strength allowed." And MSA "goes beyond regular strength. Beyond extra strength to Maximum strength." McNeilab filed suit, charging that the ads falsely claim that MSA contains more pain reliever than Extra Strength Tylenol, that the claim "maximum strength allowed" is false, and the claim MSA "contains more of the pain relievers doctors recommend most." implies that MSA is the brand of pain reliever recommended most. Plaintiff's applications for preliminary injunction and summary judgment were consolidated into a trial on the merits.

Subsequently American Home substituted "added strength" for "extra strength" but the court refused to dismiss the suit as moot[30] because McNeilab in its motion for summary judgment also challenged the claim that MSA contains the "maximum allowed" amount of pain relief and because there was not sufficient assurance that similar advertising might not be later aired.

With respect to the revised commercials, McNeilab offered no evidence of consumer reaction. The court agreed "that the change in terminology does not alter the *literal* meaning of the commercials"[31] but refused to conclude that "their message as perceived by viewers is unchanged."[32] With respect to the original two commercials, McNeilab argued that although the comparative claims were literally true, nevertheless they had a tendency to mislead, and offered ASI and Burke consumer studies of Tylenol users to establish that they received a false message of superiority. Although a Professor of consumer research and

---

28. *Id.* at 169.
29. 207 USPQ 573 (S.D.N.Y. 1980).
30. The court noted that it would be appropriate to dismiss as moot a suit for injunctive relief where the offending conduct has ceased and there is no reasonable expectation that it will resume.
31. 207 USPQ at 586.
32. *Id.*

marketing criticized the studies as deficient on various grounds and the commercial as "terribly poor", the court was not impressed with his testimony and found that consumers perceived the commercials as suggesting that MSA "is a more powerful analgesic than Extra Strength Tylenol, which it is not."[33]

Judge Lasker's discussion of the role of defendant's intent is significant as the first false advertising case to explore the effect of intent. Analogizing to the 'trade dress' cases, the court found that AHP set out to advertise MSA as unique, drawing upon such evidence as "copy strategy" and in-house communication from the medical director to its Vice-President for new products. Proof that the advertiser intended to communicate a misleading claim was held to be evidence in a false advertising case that that claim was communicated.

The court held, further, that MSA could not be advertised as the maximum strength allowed since that claim implied specific approval by FDA. The FDA proposed monograph did set forth the dose as the outer limit for nonprescription use, but MSA's product labeling did not conform to the labeling requirements proposed in the monograph for such dosage. Hence, Judge Lasker reasoned that use of this claim in advertising was false.

ASSORTED OBSERVATIONS

Even an unsuccessful advertising campaign, which may run but a season and fail to persuade purchase, exposes the advertiser to risk. Aside from the day to day activities of the NAD[34], the NAB and the Broadcast Standards and Practices departments of the networks, whose determinations may prevent the airing of the advertising or whose preliminary objections may later surface as evidence,[35] the FTC and the competition stand ready to pounce upon the advertiser who would vaunt his wares over those of his competitor.

A litigation involving comparative advertising is likely to search out and scrutinize all market research and copy testing conducted by the advertiser and its advertising agency. The state of that art is such that each side of the fray can generally find some support in the research for its position. Even the "quick and dirty" study, conducted to gain a preliminary reading on some copy point, may be in for close examination.[36]

---

33. *Id.* at 583.
34. The National Advertising Division of the Council of Better Business Bureaus.
35. See, *e.g., McNeilab, supra,* at 585.
36. *In the Matter of Bristol-Myers Co. and Ogilvy & Mather, Inc.,* 85 FTC 688 (1975).

The real key to succeeding in a comparative advertising case, where the alleged falsehood is not patent, lies in carefully conducted, well designed studies. There has been a demonstrable reluctance on the part of the judiciary to apply its own opinion or the opinion of expert witnesses to determine the pivotal issue of what the consumer perceives or retains from the advertising, hence consumer studies are the *sine qua non*. The possible studies come in infinite varieties and sizes. In addition to those designed to directly test consumer reaction, attitudes and images, others can be designed to point up flaws in the design of studies conducted by the adversary or to disprove their results or to establish their effect, as market penetration studies.

The problems, expense and risk of a private litigation in a comparative advertising case become even greater in an FTC proceeding. While a court in private litigation will limit an injunction to the involved claims, the FTC has a form of "broad order" which can be applied to all products in the same overall category (such as all over-the-counter pharmaceuticals) and can mandate proof for all future adversiting claims, which may to the uninitiated seem innocuous but generally imposes standards higher than prevailing industry standards,[37] with the result that the advertiser is placed at a competitive disadvantage. Such FTC practice may necessitate judicial redress to limit the order so that it reasonably relates to the wrongdoing.[38] The difficulties of prevailing on appeal are increased by the size of the record and the specialized subject matter in which the administrative tribunal may be perceived as having special expertise. Then too, the unsuccessful FTC respondent does not reach the court until after the hearing before the Administrative Law Judge and appeal to the Commission, and then the appeal to court is confined to the printed record.

Before leaping into the complex of comparative advertising, the advertiser may be well advised to consider the hazards and weigh them against the anticipated benefits of the campaign.

---

37. Administrative Law Judge Montgomery K. Hyun, in *In the Matter of Sterling Drug Inc.*, Dkt. 8919, 1/30/81, recognized "the close questions of policy involving certain competing considerations which demand a careful deliberation regarding Bayer's superior quality claims." Thus in a thoughtful footnote he stated that ". . . a legal requirement that every comparative pharmaceutical quality claim be substantiated by well-controlled clinical trials may have a chilling effect upon true and honest claims of product quality, and be tantamount to unlawful prior restraint on commercial speech. Finally, it may run counter to the Commission's established policy of encouraging free flow of significant product information." (slip op. at 331)

38. *Beneficial Corp.* v. *F.T.C.*, 542 F.2d 611 (3d Cir. 1976), *cert. denied*, 430 U.S. 983 (1977); *American Home Products Corp.* v. *F.T.C.*, 402 F.2d 232 (6th Cir. 1968).

GARY B. WILCOX

Implications of First Amendment Doctrine on Prohibition of Truthful Price Advertising Concerning Alcoholic Beverages

Gary B. Wilcox is an Assistant Professor of Advertising in the College of Communication, The University of Texas at Austin. He holds a BBA in Marketing and a MA in Communications from The University of Texas at Austin and a Ph.D. in Mass Media from Michigan State University. His articles will appear in the *Journal of Advertising* and the *1981 AAA Proceedings*.

I. INTRODUCTION

Since 1942 governmental regulation of commercial advertising has become a focus of controversy to established First Amendment doctrine.[1] An increasing number of suits have raised constitutional issues

1. See *Virginia State Board of Pharmacy v Virginia Citizens Consumer Council*, 425 U.S. 748; *Bigelow v Virginia*, 421 U.S. 809; *Bates v State Bar of Arizona*, 97 S.Ct. 2691; *Pittsburgh Press Co. v Pittsburgh Commission on Human Relations*, 413 U.S. 376; and *Valentine v Chrestensen*, 316 U.S. 52.

regarding regulation of offensive advertising,[2] false or deceptive advertising,[3] and prohibitions of price advertising for particular products or services.[4] Until recently, the majority of courts upheld such regulations under the Supreme Court's ruling in *Valentine v Chrestensen* that "purely commercial advertising" is unprotected by the First Amendment.[5]

In 1973, in *Pittsburgh Press v Pittsburgh Commission on Human Relations,*[6] the Court focused on the limited content of the speech in *Valentine* as justification for its treatment as commercial speech. The Court said: "The critical feature of the advertisement in *Valentine v Chrestensen* was that, in the Court's view, it did no more than propose a commercial transaction."[7] Lower court decisions also listed the profit motive and proposals of a transaction as factors in determining the scope of commercial speech.[8]

These criteria for identifying commercial speech seemed to be definitional expressions for the most frequently used rationale for denying protection to commercial speech. The rationale was that such speech is unrelated to the expression of opinions and grievances which the First Amendment was intended to protect.

In *Virginia State Board of Pharmacy v Virginia Citizens Consumer Council, Inc.*[9] the Court reconsidered the issue, declaring unconstitutional a statute that penalized druggists for advertising prescription drug prices. The Court held that commercial speech is not "wholly outside the protection of the First Amendment,"[10] and that it does not lack "all protection."[11] Other recent action in the First Amendment/advertising area has arisen concerning lawyers[12] and eyeglass companies[13] right to advertise truthful information.

The subject with which this paper deals concerns the advancement

---

2. *State v Cardwell*, 539 P. 2d 169.
3. *Beneficial Corp. v FTC*, 542 F. 2d 611; *FTC v National Commission on Egg Nutrition*, 517 F. 2d 485.
4. *Virginia State Board of Pharmacy; Bates, supra,* note 1.
5. 316 U.S. 52.
6. 413 U.S. 376.
7. *Valentine*, 316 U.S. 52 at 385.
8. *United States v Bob Lawrence Realty*, 474 F. 2d 115; *United States v Hunter*, 457 F. 2d 205; *Stevenson v Board of Regents of the University of Texas*, 393 F. Supp. 812.
9. 425 U.S. 748.
10. *Id.* at 761.
11. *Id.* at 762.
12. *Bates*, 97 S. Ct. 2691.
13. *California Citizen Action Group v Dept of Consumer Affairs*, 407 F. Supp. 1075.

of points raised in *Virginia*,[14] *Bates*,[15] and other First Amendment cases[16] to the issue of price advertising of alcohol products. A number of states in their desire to control the regulation of alcohol products have prohibited comparative price advertising. This ruling appears to have far reaching constitutional and economic implications. The focus of this paper presents a case for the abolishment of state prohibition of advertisements in the mass media containing specific price information for alcohol products. Issues important in the determination of the public policy such as the consumer decision process from both a behavioral and economic viewpoint as well as constitutional issues raised in recent court cases will be examined.

Organization of the Paper

This paper is organized into five sections. A general background of advertising and the First Amendment is discussed in the introduction. In the second section, the consumer decision process is examined from a behavioral point of view. Section three deals with the economic aspects of advertising and briefly an econometric consumer decision model. Section four presents a review of the First Amendment/advertising issue focusing on the most precedent setting decisions. In the final section, the implications for public policy treatment of alcohol price advertising are examined.

II. CONSUMER BEHAVIOR AND PUBLIC POLICY

The principle of individual choice underlies basic economic theories and practices of many societies in the world. A thorough understanding of public policy therefore cannot exist without assumptions about how consumers choose to spend their time, money or energy. To design public policy that will successfully mediate consumer and societal problems requires an indepth understanding of the needs, desires, and motivations of the consumers for whom the policies are developed.

A study of consumer actions from the decision process perspective provides important information for both marketing and public policy decision making. Knowledge about components such as belief, attitudes, and relative importance of information sources are useful in

14. 425 U.S. 748.
15. 97 S. Ct. 2691.
16. *Carey v Population Services International*, 52 L. Ed. 2d 675; *California Citizen Action Group v Dept of Consumer Affairs*, 407 F. Supp. 1075.

designing product marketing strategies as well as public policy directions.

Generally, there are five important parts of consumer decision making behavior — problem recognition, search, alternative evaluation, choice, and outcomes. Problem recognition occurs when an individual perceives a difference between an ideal state of affairs and the actual state at any moment in time. Once a problem is recognized, the consumer must then assess the available alternatives for action. This assessment includes processing of both internal and external information. Once information has been received, the consumer then evaluates the alternatives and arrives at a purchase decision. Finally, choice and outcomes of the choice complete the decision process model of consumer behavior.[17]

The part of this model that is most relevant to the public policy issue discussed in this paper is search. Generally, search results when existing beliefs and attitudes are found to be inadequate. More often than not though, search does not precede the majority of consumer purchases. For example, a past solution to a recognized problem can be recalled and implemented.[18] However, search may represent a motivated decision to seek additional inputs. In general, the decision to search, as well as the extent of search, depends upon the consumer's perception of the value to be gained in comparison with the costs of obtaining and using that information.[19]

There are several factors that can serve to motivate search: (1) the quality and quantity of existing information, (2) the ability to recall that information, (3) perceived risk, and (4) confidence in decision making ability.[20] First, the more a person knows, the lower the propensity to search, all things being equal. Research findings support that search is much less probable when a product has been bought repeatedly over time.[21] Similarly, the greater the number of brands of the generic product that have been purchased previously, the lower likelihood of search.[22] Therefore, both the presence and the extent of search vary inversely with the length and breadth of experience.

17. Engel, James F. Blackwell, Roger D. Kollat, David T., *Consumer Behavior* 3rd edition, 1978, pp. 23-27; Woodside, Arch. G. Sheth, Jagdish N., Bennett, Peter D., *Consumer and Industrial Buying Behavior,* 1977, 99. 35-67.
18. Katona, George, *Psychological Analysis of Economic Behavior,* 1951, p. 47.
19. Engel, p. 238.
20. Engel, p. 239.
21. Katona, George, *The Mass Consumption Society,* 1964, pp. 289-290; Newman, Joseph, W. and Staelin, Richard, "Prepurchase Information Seeking for New Cars and Major Household Appliances," *Journal of Marketing Research,* August, 1972, pp. 249-257.
22. Katona, p. 290; Newman, p. 249-257.

The ability to recall stored information depends in part on the degree to which the present problem is perceived to be similar to those which have been encountered before.[23] For example, in simple habitual choice situations, a consumer may make a decision immediately, with no need for additional information beyond that needed to actually choose the item (recall of the brand name or recognition of the package).

Information search is also a way of reducing risk to acceptable levels.[24] Generally speaking, the greater the degree of perceived risk, the greater the degree of propensity to search. The consumer search for and handling of information will be directed toward minimizing the potential risks.[25] If the risk is low however, it would be perfectly reasonable for the consumer to ignore information no matter how relevant that information may appear to the policy maker or marketer. The confidence that a consumer has in his decision making ability is a determinate of the amount of information sought. When confidence is low, search obviously is more likely.[26]

In making a choice, the consumer may retrieve information from memory, and in some cases search for further information if that in memory is not sufficient. Initially, search may be internal, with memory being searched for relevant information. Various degrees of internal search are possible, ranging from virtually automatic responses in habitual choice situations to more extensive searches of what is in memory. In many cases, the initial search may not be exhaustive or comprehensive — the purpose being to ascertain what is not known and to provide a guide for external search.[27]

External search is the acquisition of information from sources other than memory, such as friends, packages or advertisements. It has been a difficult problem to determine the relative importance of various information sources from the empirical studies undertaken to date.

23. May, Fredrick E., "Adaptive Behavior in Automobile Brand Choices," *Journal of Marketing Research*, February, 1969, pp. 62-65; Swan, John W., "Experimental Analysis of Predecision Information Seeking," *Journal of Marketing Research*, May, 1969, pp. 192-197.
24. Bauer, Raymond A., "Consumer Behavior as Risk Taking," *Dynamic Marketing for a Changing World*, Robert S. Hancock ed., 1960, pp. 389-398.
25. Green, Paul E., "Consumer Use of Information", *On Knowing the Consumer*, Joseph Newman ed., 1966, pp. 67-80; Cunningham, Scott M., "Perceived Risk as a Factor in Product Oriented Word of Mouth Behavior; A First Step," *Reflections on Progress in Marketing*, L. George Smith ed. 1964, pp. 229-38.
26. Engel, p. 241.
27. Bettman, James R., *An Information Processing Theory of Consumer Choice*, 1979, pp. 28-31.

Generally, these studies have been classified according to the type of methodology used: (1) effectiveness and (2) exposure or non-exposure as a criterion of effectiveness.[28]

The data reveal, first of all, that consumers rarely rely exclusively on one source. Rather, search tends to be a cumulative process in that those who seek information from one source also turn to others and vice versa.[29] This finding would suggest that the various media are complementary rather than competitive.

If exposure is used as the criterion of importance, the marketer-dominated sources (advertising, point-of-purchase, and personal selling) are usually preponderant. The general mass media also rank well on this criterion in some cases. This suggests that the mass media, whether dominated by the marketer or not perform an informing function.[30] They play an important role in providing data about the availability and attributes of various alternatives.[31] This informing function generally prevails regardless of the type of purchase or choice that is being made.

When effectiveness is used as the criterion, the nonmarketer-dominated sources, especially word-of-mouth assume the primary role. Contact with friends and relatives typically assumes a legitimatizing or evaluating function because of greater credibility and clarity. Generally speaking, consumers often use friends and relatives for information about quality, but personal sources such as these will seldom perform an informing function about price, particularly if the price of the product is high.[32]

Advertisements generally are consulted to learn about such product attributes as price and color, to compare various brands on the basis of these attributes, to visualize the product in use or to learn about possible financing arrangements. This informative role of advertising is a vital one taking on increasing significance by allowing the consumer to economize on the external search process.[33] Assuming that the infor-

28. Engel, p. 250.
29. Katz, Eli, "The Two Step Flow of Communication: An Up-to-Date Report on an Hypothesis," *Public Opinion Quarterly,* vol. 20, 1957, pp. 61-78; Wilkining, Eugene A., "Joint Decision Making as a Function of Status and Role," *American Sociological Review,* vol. 23, 1958, pp. 187-192.
30. Legrand, Bruce, Udell, Jon, "Consumer Behavior in the Market Place," *Journal of Retailing,* Fall, 1964, pp. 32-40.
31. Berning, Carol A. Kohn, Jacoby, Jacob, "Patterns of Information Acquisition in New Product Purchases," *Journal of Consumer Research,* Sept., 1974, pp. 18-22; Robinson, John P., "Mass Communication and Information Diffusion," *Current Perspectives in Mass Communications Research,* G. Kline and P.J. Tichenor eds., 1972.
32. Engel, p. 250.
33. Engel, p. 260.

mation provided is relevant in terms of the consumer's evaluative criteria, advertising may bring about certain changes in beliefs and attitudes. However, there are instances in which advertising will play a major decisive role in the decision. At times, for example, the consumer may have decided to purchase a product and will use advertising for a price comparison of the several acceptable brands. Price advertising then will trigger a sale and this is its primary role. [34]

III. ECONOMIC ASPECTS OF ADVERTISING

Over the years the role advertising has played in the economic environment of the United States has become an area of much criticism. Economists have generally agreed that advertising is economically wasteful. Most of these critics feel advertising can be wasteful in several ways: (1) by adding unnecessarily to costs, (2) by an inefficient use of the nation's resources, (3) by encouraging excessive competition and (4) by persuading consumers to buy items they do not need. [35]

Despite the cries of these social critics, advertising acts as a key element in the economic system by providing relevant information to the consumer and thereby helping him make many of his shopping decisions. Advertising plays a major informational role in the economy because: (1) products are available in such wide varieties, (2) new products are offered in such great numbers, and (3) existing products must be called to the attention of new customers who enter the market as a result of expansion in three areas—income, population, and tastes. An advertisement may communicate the availability, price, quality and other attributes, thereby permitting the consumers to make a better choice than if they had to seek the information from each individual seller. [36]

The information role of advertising has been summarized by Stigler:

> . . .Under competition, the main tasks of a seller are to inform potential buyers of his existence, his line of goods, and his prices. Since both sellers and buyers change over time, since people forget information once acquired, and since new products appear, the existence of sellers must be continually advertised. . . [37]

---

34. Engel, p. 261.
35. Howard, John A., and Hulbert, James, "Advertising and the Public Interest," *Journal of Advertising Research*, December, 1974, p. 3.
36. Scherer, F.M., *Industrial Market Structure and Economic Performance*, 1970, p. 325.
37. Stigler, George J., *The Theory of Price*, 1966, p. 200.

He continues to point out that ". . .information is a valuable resource, which reduces drastically the cost of search."[38]

By allowing consumers to economize on search and to locate low-priced sellers more readily, advertising may tend to lower prices to the consumers. It may also lower prices by allowing sellers or producers to economize on other merchandizing costs and to take advantage of economies of scale.[39]

An economic model dealing with the variables that make up the total of a good may help shed more light on the consumer use of information. The full cost of purchase (C_f) of a good or service to a consumer includes not only the cost of the item itself (C_g) but the cost of knowledge (C_k) concerning the location of sales outlets and prices and the cost of time and transportation (C_t) required to purchase the item: $C_f = C_g + C_k + C_t$. These components of full cost are partially dependent on each other. For a given frequency distribution of retail prices offered in the market, the distribution of prices paid (C_g) will depend upon the extent of consumers' knowledge of the alternative prices available and the cost of time and transportation. Past studies have shown that both the mean and the dispersion of prices paid generally decrease as the extent of search increases.[40]

As advertising increases consumers knowledge of alternative prices offered by retailers in the market, it will tend to decrease the mean and dispersion of prices paid. In general, large-volume, low-priced sellers are dependent upon drawing consumers from a wide area and consequently need to inform their potential customers of the advantages of coming to them. If advertising is prohibited, they may not be able to generate the necessary sales to maintain the low prices. In such a situation, the cost of disseminating information to consumers will more than offset the economies of scale that may be present.[41]

IV. FIRST AMENDMENT/ADVERTISING CASES

The Supreme Court did not consider the First Amendment status of commercial speech until 1942 when in *Valentine v Chrestensen*,[42] the Court held that the amendment's protection did not extend to commer-

38. Stigler, p. 200.
39. Benham, Lee, "The Effect of Advertising on the Price of Eyeglasses," *Journal of Law and Economics,* October, 1972, p. 337.
40. Benham, p. 338, Stigler, George J., "The Economics of Information," *Journal of Political Economy,* 1961, p. 213.
41. Benham, p. 338-339.
42. 316 U.S. 52. *cf Bleistein v Donaldson Lithography Co.* 188 U.S. 239, 251 on allowing advertising material to be protected under the Patent & Copyright clause of the Constitution.

cial speech. The plaintiff in *Valentine* had distributed handbills advertising tours of a submarine until police informed him that he was violating an ordinance that prohibited public distribution of commercial advertisements.[43] The promoter then distributed a revised handbill with the tour advertisement on the one side and a protest against the city's ordinance on the reverse. The Court found this supposed political protest to be merely a plan to evade the ordinance and suggested that "purely commercial advertising" was not protected by the First Amendment. The Court held that the Constitution imposed no restraint upon the regulation of commercial advertising in public ways.

Perhaps the most influential aspect of *Valentine* arose from the Court's casual reference to the Circuit Court's opinion: "The court below. . .adverts to the difficulty of apportioning. . .the contents of the communication as between what is of public interest and what is for private profit."[44] Assuming that the commercial message was not of public interest, the Court found it unnecessary to attempt apportionment because it concluded that the plaintiff had added the protest for the sole purpose of evading the ordinance.[45]

In the decisions that followed, the dichotomy between types of expression was a controversial one. The Court distinguished *Valentine* in order to protect speech more often than it relied upon the case to uphold regulation.[46] The importance accorded to motive and to the lower court's distinction between speech of public interest and speech of a commercial nature proved to be *Valentine's* most durable application.[47] More than thirty years after *Valentine* was decided, the Court characterized the case as upholding "a reasonable regulation of the manner in which commercial advertising could be distributed."[48]

In *Bigelow v Virginia,*[49] the Court could have shed additional light on the ambiguity between commercial speech and other speech. It had left open that possibility in *Pittsburgh Press.*[50] However, the Court in *Bigelow* continued the distinction but afforded more First Amendment protection to some commercial speech than it had formerly given.

---

43. *Id.* at 53.
44. *Id.* at 55.
45. *Id.* at 55.
46. *Virginia*, 425 U.S. 748 at 759.
47. Sbaratta, Rosemarie, "Yes, FTC, There is a *Virginia:* The Impact of *Virginia State Board of Pharmacy v Virginia Citizens Consumer Council, Inc.* on the Federal Trade Commission's Regulation of Misleading Advertising," *Boston University Law Review,* November, 1977, pp. 834-35.
48. *Bigelow,* 421 U.S. 809 at 819.
49. 421 U.S. 809.
50. 413 U.S. 376.

Jeffery C. Bigelow, a managing editor of the *Virginia Weekly,* was convicted for violating a Virginia statute which made it a misdemeanor for any person by advertisement to encourage or prompt the procuring of abortions. His conviction was reversed by the Supreme Court which held that merely because an advertisement is labeled commercial speech does not mean it is stripped all First Amendment safeguards, as implied in *Valentine.* [51]

The Court formulated the standard for determining the constitutionality of commercial speech regulation as "assessing the First Amendment interest at stake and weighing it against the public interest allegedly served by the regulation." [52] Included in this standard is the view that the different types of commercial speech have different First Amendment value, and that the magnitude of governmental interest sufficient to justify an advertising regulation will vary according to the value of the advertising. The Court stated:

> The diverse motives, means, and messages of advertising may make speech "commercial" in widely varying degrees. We need not decide here the extent to which constitutional protection is afforded commercial advertising under all circumstances and in the face of all kinds of regulation. [53]

In determining whether the advertisement fell within the area of protected speech, the Court noted the factual material of interest to the public contained in the ad. [54] "Public interest" was meant to include either those items in which the public is interested, or those which the public should know. Such speech retains some degree of constitutional protection which must be weighed against the state's interest in regulating the particular advertisement. [55] In summation, the Court in *Bigelow* concentrated on the content of the advertisement and found that it contained items of sufficient value to warrant protection.

In *Virginia State Board of Pharmacy v Virginia Citizens Consumer Council,* [56] the Court confronted a statute that imposed sanctions upon pharmacists who advertised drug prices. The plaintiffs, who characterized themselves as a group of prescription drug consumers sought an in-

51. 421 U.S. 809 at 822.
52. *Id.* at 826.
53. *Id.* at 826.
54. *Id.* at 822.
55. Sheridan, David, "Commercial Speech: The Supreme Court Sends Another *Valentine* to Advertisers," *Buffalo Law Review,* Vol. 25, 1976, pp. 742-745.
56. 425 U.S. 748.

junction against inforcement of the statute, claiming that it violated the First and Fourteenth Amendments[57] and their "right to know."[58] A three-judge District Court granted the injunction, declaring the statute unconstitutional; the Supreme Court affirmed.[59] The Defendants, Virginia State Board of Pharmacy, replied that such advertising was mere "commercial speech" undeserving of any First Amendment protection and therefore subject to regulation.[60] The Supreme Court held that purely commercial speech in the form of truthful information about entirely lawful activity may not be completely suppressed by a state,[61] that such speech receives the protection of the First and Fourteenth Amendments,[62] and that a reciprocal First Amendment "right to know"[63] exists for consumers as recipients of such speech.

The Court explained that, although an advertiser's motive may be purely economic, the societal and individual interests in commercial speech justify its protection. For the consumer, the personal interest in the product advertised may be greater than the interest in political debate.[64] For society, commercial speech is "indispensable to the proper allocation of resources in a free enterprise system and to the formation of intelligent opinions as to how that system ought to be regulated or altered."[65] The Court noted that a factory's existence might depend upon its ability to advertise, and "the practices in a single factory may have economic repercussions upon a whole region and affect widespread systems of marketing."[66] The majority concluded its argument by explicitly recognizing that commercial speech and political speech further the same ends:

> Therefore, even if the First Amendment were thought
> to be primarily an instrument to enlighten public
> decision-making in a democracy we could not say that
> the free flow of information does not serve that goal.[67]

The Court went on to examine and discuss the competing interests raised in the case. The Court noted that the consumer's interest in low prices through the free flow of advertising information might often be

---

57. *Id.* at 761.
58. *Id.* at 757.
59. *Id.* at 748.
60. *Chrestensen,* 316 U.S. 52.
61. 425 U.S. 748 at 760.
62. *Id.* at 761.
63. *Id.* at 757.
64. *Id.* at 763.
65. *Id.* at 765.
66. *Id.* at 763.
67. *Id.* at 765.

stronger on a daily level than in constitutionally protected speech on political matter, especially among the old and sick who spend a greater share of their income on prescription drugs.[68]

In deciding that commercial speech should not as a whole be seen as having no public function to justify its expression, the Court argued that it would be difficult to draw a line between advertising on subjects only of public interest and advertising important to self-government.[69] Even if an ad were lacking public interest that was immediately discernible, the Court suggested that almost any subject could be considered as having a public interest element, and if not, "there are few to which such an element could not be added."[70] The Court also felt informational advertising about any subject was important if for no other reason than affecting the personal economic decisions made as a result of exposure to such information.[71] The Court suggested that the proper allocation of resources will come about only through the greatest informational exposure possible, and likewise, the information indispensable to the success of the free enterprise system must be indispensable to the government in a free enterprise economy.[72] Therefore, commercial speech should be seen as ultimately containing a public rather than a private character.[73]

The judicial balancing that followed rivaled the state's interest in maintaining high professional standards against the combined weights of the consumer's First Amendment right to know, the public's interest in the most advantageous allocation of resources, and the advertiser's interest in free speech when truthful information about entirely lawful activity is being conveyed.[74] The Pharmacy Board's belief that low cost, high volume unprofessional drug retailers would consume the market was recognized as a possibility.[75] But, the assumption that people in a democratic society will be the better protectors of their own interests through open channels of communication was felt to be a sufficient counterbalancing issue.[76] In deciding the case, the Court felt that the statute must fail because it denied consumers the chance to decide for themselves.[77]

The Court carefully limited its holding so that states may continue

68. *Id.* at 763.
69. *Id.* at 765.
70. *Id.* at 764.
71. *Id.* at 765.
72. *Id.* at 765.
73. *Id.* at 765.
74. *Id.* at 766-770.
75. *Id.* at 769.
76. *Id.* at 770.
77. *Id.* at 770.

to regulate advertising under certain conditions. Advertising regulations made without reference to content and which are "mere time, place and manner restrictions" while allowing for "ample alternative channels for communication" were sanctioned as long as they serve "a significant governmental interest."[78] In addition, the state's ability to regulate false advertising was re-affirmed.[79] Furthermore, the decision did not apply to "the special problems of the electronic broadcast media."[80] The question of a state's power to regulate price advertising by other professions was particularly reserved since filling the prescription was more akin to dispensing a product than providing a professional service.[81]

Following this decision, the California District Court ruled in *California Citizen Action Group v Department of Consumer Affairs,*[82] the prohibition of advertising of prices and places of sales for eyeglasses unconstitutional on the grounds of the consumers right to receive information. The Court stated, "the right to receive and have truthful information of comparative prices and where to buy corrective eyeglasses for the furtherance of his health and welfare is protected by the First Amendment."[83]

The Supreme Court, following *Virginia* continued to provide First Amendment protection to purely commercial speech. In *Carey v Population Services International,* the Court rejected as unconstitutional a New York statute which made it a crime for anyone to advertise the availability and price of contraceptives.[84]

Most recently the Supreme Court has examined prohibitions against lawyer advertising. In *Bates v State Bar of Arizona,* attorneys practicing in Arizona placed an advertisement in a local newspaper listing their fees for certain legal servcies.[85] The Arizona State Bar found that the attorneys had violated the state bar's absolute prohibition of lawyer's advertising. The Arizona Supreme Court upheld the finding of the Arizona State Bar and First Amendment challenges to the prohibition.[86] On appeal, the Supreme Court held that commercial speech in the form of a truthful advertisement concerning the availability and prices of routine legal services is protected by the First Amend-

---

78. *Id.* at 770-71.
79. *Id.* at 776-779.
80. *Id.* at 773.
81. *Id.* at 773-75.
82. 407 F. Supp. 1075.
83. *Id.* at 1079.
84. 52 L. Ed. 2d 675.
85. 97 S. Ct. 2691.
86. Arizona Rev. Stat., Sup. Ct. R 29 (a) (West Supp. 1977-78).

ment from absolute prohibition by a state.[87]

In *Bates,* the Supreme Court began with the assumption that *Virginia Pharmacy* would be the controlling case unless the Arizona Bar Association could show that "the differences among professions might bring different constitutional considerations into play,"[88] i.e. that lawyers advertising presented a greater potential for harm than pharmacists' advertising. Pointing out the varied nature of attorney's services, the bar association emphasized that even the most routine legal problems present factors unique to each case. Thus, advertised prices for specific services would be inherently misleading, since costs could not be accurately established prior to consultation with the client.[89] The bar association also claimed that because of the prearrangement of prices the services provided by the attorneys might not precisely fit the clients needs.[90] The Court concluded, however, that certain legal services, especially those advertised by these attorneys are so routine that their prices may accurately be advertised.[91]

Using arguments advanced in *Virginia,*[92] the bar association predicted that advertising would jeopardize professional standards[93] and produce undesirable economic effects.[94] Advertising, the concluded, would commercialize legal practice, undermine attorneys' self-respect, and overemphasize profit orientation at the expense of service. Ultimately, the clients' trust in their attorneys would be diminished.[95] Acknowledging the possibility that some advertising costs would inevitably be passed to consumers, the Court felt it was at least equally likely that advertising would lower prices by stimulating competition.[96] The Court concluded:

> Although it is true that the effect of advertising of the price of services has not been demonstrated, there is revealing evidence with regard to products; where consumers have the benefit of price advertising retail prices often are dramatically lower than they would be without advertising.[97]

87. 97 S. Ct. 2691. See "Problems in Lawyer Advertising" by Judge Aron Steuer, *Communications and the Law,* Vol. 1, No. 2, Spring 1979, p. 69.
88. *Id.* at 2700.
89. *Id.* at 2703-4.
90. *Id.* at 2706.
91. *Id.* at 2703.
92. *Virginia,* 425 U.S. 748 at 766-769.
93. 97 S. Ct. 2691 at 2701.
94. *Id.* at 2705.
95. *Id.* at 2701.
96. *Id.* at 2706.
97. *Id.* at 2706.

In addition, the majority recognized an additional benefit that would occur from price advertising by attorneys — since the use of the legal profession by certain large segments of the population has been minimal, advertising would encourage the assertion of valid claims by eliminating potential clients fear of high costs and the inability to find qualified lawyers.[98]

Following *Virginia,* the majority in *Bates* reaffirmed the principle justifying First Amendment protection of advertising: advertising is valuable in a free market economy, serving both the society and the individual in promoting the efficient allocation of resources and in bringing buyers and sellers together in the marketplace.[99] Because of its intrinsic value, advertising should not be absolutely prohibited unless the dangers created by the advertising are clearly greater than the harm done by its prohibition. Absent such a showing, the First Amendment forbids prohibition.[100]

Adopting the balancing approach of *Virginia,*[101] the Court's inquiry did not focus upon the importance of the state interests in question, nor upon the seriousness of the dangers presented by attorneys' advertising, but rather upon whether the dangers of advertising were real, based upon logic and empirical evidence, or illusory. The essence of the holding was not that consumers' interests outweighed those of the state, but that, based on empirical evidence,[102] a limited amount of legal advertising would be more beneficial to consumers than the state's absolute prohibition of such advertising.

V. CONCLUSIONS

The ambiguity tied to the First Amendment/advertising issue from its beginnings seemed to have been lessened somewhat by the recent decisions of the Supreme Court. By tracing the recent rulings and examining their rationale the general position of advertising and the First Amendment can be ascertained. Generally speaking, the Court has struck down regulations prohibiting the dissemination of commercial speech about truthful, lawful activity concerning products and services. The Court feels that this type of information is essential to a healthy economic system and places the importance on the right of the consumer to receive above the authority of the states to regulate such infor-

98. *Id.* at 2705.
99. *Id.* at 2699.
100. *Id.* at 2699; *Virginia,* 425 U.S. 748 at 770.
101. 425 U.S. 748 at 766-769.
102. 97 S. Ct. 2691 at 2702; 2706.

mation. The use of empirical evidence to determine the benefits of the advertising to consumers as noted in *Virginia* and *Bates* also suggests the increasing importance the Court will place on this type of material in future litigation.

The Court does make a distinction, however, between products and services. In general, the Court seems to acknowledge the right to truthfully advertise any legal product. Judgment has been reserved on the application of such a broad mandate concerning services referring instead to a case by case analysis.

It can be assumed that the states have a valid and important interest in regulating the advertising of alcoholic beverages. There is no question that they should be allowed to regulate the time, manner, and place of such advertisements. [103] Even conceding these interests, there seems to be no satisfying reason that would compel the states to completely suppress the dissemination of truthful information about price. Indeed, the states generally allow other types of advertising for alcoholic beverages not only in the print media but the broadcast media as well. This surely does not benefit the economic interests of the consumer as would more informative price advertising. Empirical evidence in both the consumer behavior and economic literature suggests that by allowing the consumer the opportunity to compare prices via the print media the cost of search, time, transportation, and ultimately the cost of the product will be reduced.

A majority of the states do not prohibit price advertising of alcoholic beverages, and at least one study has concluded that there is no direct relationship between advertising and consumption. [104] However, even if the states have a legitimate interest in protecting the health and morals of its citizens, this interest can be fulfilled by regulating the time, manner, and place of the advertisements for price of alcoholic beverages. Proper regulation could also be aided by voluntary self-restraints imposed by media on these advertisements. Thus temperance can be encouraged and sensibilities be protected through readily identifiable means that are far less drastic than total prohibition.

There are two important constitutional principles involved in these regulations that are not limited just to the subject of liquor. First, the right of every merchant, large or small, to fairly and honestly advertise his or her product is prohibited. Second, and perhaps more important-

---

103. *Virginia*, see footnote #78.
104. The Joint Committee of the States to Study Alcoholic Beverage Laws, *Uniform Standards for Advertising of Alcoholic Beverages in Newspapers and Magazines*, 1975, pp. 70-75.

ly, the rights of thousands of residents to read, to see the claims of these merchants, and to make informed decisions about the quality of the merchandise offered and the fairness of the price charged is being denied.

In view of the recent decisions of the Supreme Court of the United States, the present regulations in the states prohibiting truthful price advertising are too broad and restrictive to be considered constitutional. A re-examination of these regulations is in order to ensure the most efficient functioning of the American economic system and the proper application of the First Amendment of the United States Constitution.

EXHIBIT I

STATES PROHIBITING PRICE ADVERTISING OF ALCOHOLIC BEVERAGES IN NEWSPAPERS AND MAGAZINES

Delaware	New Jersey
Georgia	North Carolina
Michigan	Ohio
Minnesota	Pennsylvania
New Hampshire	Rhode Island

Source: United States Brewers Association Inc., Legal Department Memo — Special Information on Advertising, 12/79.

BIBLIOGRAPHY

Bauer, Raymond A., "Consumer Behavior as Risk Taking," *Dynamic Marketing for a Changing World,* Robert S. Hancock ed., 1960.

Benham, Lee, "The Effects of Advertising on the Price of Eyeglasses," *Journal of Law and Economics,* October, 1972.

Berning, Carol A. Kohn, Jacoby, Jacob, "Patterns of Information Acquisition in New Product Purchases," *Journal of Consumer Research,* September, 1974.

Bettman, James R., *An Information Processing Theory of Consumer Choice,* 1979.

Cunningham, Scott M., "Perceived Risk as a Factor in Product Oriented Word of Mouth Behavior: A First Step," *Reflections on Progress in Marketing,* L. George Smith ed. 1964.

Distilled Spirits Council of the United States, *Summary of State Laws and Regulations Relating to Distilled Spirits,* 1977.

Engel, James F. Blackwell, Roger D. Kollat, David T., *Consumer Behavior,* 3rd Edition, 1978.

Fitzpatrick, Richard, State Representative 48th District, State of Michigan, *Memo to Stanley Thayer, Chairperson, Liquor Control Commission;* Interpretation of the 21st Amendment, September 5, 1979.

Fitzpatrick, Richard, Personal Interview, *First Amendment Issue/Advertising of Price for Alcoholic Beverages in Michigan;* November 12, 1980, State Capital—Lansing, Michigan.

Fitzpatrick, Richard, Testimony given Before the Liquor Control Commission, September 5, 1979.

Green, Paul E., "Consumer Use of Information," *On Knowing the Consumer,* Joseph Newman, ed. 1966.

Howard, John A., and Hulbert, James, "Advertising and the Public Interest," *Journal of Advertising Research,* December, 1974.

The Joint Committee of the States to Study Alcoholic Beverage Laws, *Uniform Standards for Advertising of Alcoholic Beverages in Newspapers and Magazines,* 1975.

Katona, George, *Psychological Analysis of Economic Behavior,* 1951.

Katona, George, *The Mass Consumption Society,* 1964.

Katz, Eli, "The Two Step Flow of Communication: An Up-to-Date Report on an Hypothesis," *Public Opinion Quarterly,* vol. 20, 1957.

Legrand, Bruce, Udell, Jon, "Consumer Behavior in the Market Place," *Journal of Retailing,* Fall, 1964.

May, Fred, "Adaptive Behavior in Automobile Brand Choices," *Journal of Marketing Research,* February, 1969.

Martin, Leonard W., "Constitutional Law—First Amendment Protection Extended to Price Advertising by Attorneys," *Tulane Law Review,* vol. 52, 1978.

Merril, Thomas W., "First Amendment Protection for Commercial Advertising: The New Constitutional Doctrine," *The University of Chicago Law Review,* vol. 44, 1976.

Nelson, Phillip, "Advertising as Information," *Journal of Political Economy,* vol. 81, no. 4, July/August, 1974.

Newman, Joseph, W. and Staelin, Richard, "Prepurchase Information Seeking for New Cars and Major Household Appliances," *Journal of Marketing Research,* August, 1972.

Robinson, John P., "Mass Communication and Information Diffusion," *Current Perspectives in Mass Communications Research,* G. Kline and P.J. Tichenor eds. 1972.

Sbaratta, Rosemarie, "Yes, FTC, There is a *Virginia:* The Impact of *Virginia State Board of Pharmacy v Virginia Citizens Consumer Council, Inc.* on the Federal Trade Commission's Regulation of Misleading Advertising," *Boston University Law Review,* November, 1977.

Scherer, F.M. *Industrial Market Structure and Economic Performance,* 1970.

Sheridan, David, "Commercial Speech: The Supreme Court Sends Another *Valentine* to Advertisers," *Buffalo Law Review,* vol. 25, 1976.

Steiner, Robert L., "Does Advertising Lower Consumer Prices?" *Journal of Marketing,* vol. 37, October, 1973.

Stigler, George J., *The Theory of Price,* 1966.

Swan, John E., "Experimental Analysis of Predecision Information Seeking," *Journal of Marketing Research,* May, 1969.

United States Brewers Association Inc., *Legal Department Memo—Special Information on Advertising,* 12/79.

Wallendorf, Melanie and Gerald Zaltman, *Readings in Consumer Behavior: Individuals, Groups, and Organizations,* 1979.

Ward, Scott, and Robinson, Thomas S., *Consumer Behavior: Theoretical Sources,* 1973.

Wilkining, Eugene A., "Joint Decision Making as a Function of Status and Role," *American Sociological Review,* vol. 23, 1958.

Woodside, A.G., Sheth, J.N., Bennett, Peter D., *Consumer and Industrial Buying Behavior,* 1977.

Zuckman, Harvey and Gaynes, Martin J., *Mass Communication Law in a Nutshell,* 1977.

A. ANDREW GALLO

False and Comparative Advertising Under Section 43(a) of the Lanham Trademark Act*

A. Andrew Gallo is an attorney with the
Law Department, Litigation Section, of
Exxon Company, U.S.A., Houston, Texas.
He received his J.D., with Order of the
Coif Honors, from the Marshall-Wythe
School o: Law, The College of William
and Mary in Virginia in 1985. He
graduated from Hofstra University, Hemp-
stead, New York, in 1982.

Comparative advertising is expanding rapidly in both the business and legal arenas. Hardly a station-break passes without some celebrity, model or even little old lady popping on the screen and plugging someone's product at the expense of someone else's product. In 1982, fully twenty-five percent of all ads made product comparisons.[1] In 1973, comparative ads made up only three percent of all advertising.[2]

The most important issue addressed in this article is whether consumers should have standing to sue under section 43(a) of the Lanham Trademark Act. An analysis of the elements of a cause of action follows, including the important determination of whether an ad is:

(1) false on its face;

(2) misleading due to public perception of the ad; or

(3) deceptive as a result of defendant using faulty methodology in tests, leading to deception of the viewing public.

*The author would like to thank Steven L. Schooner, U.S. Army J.A.G. Corps., for his assistance and perseverance in making this article possible.

1. The State, Columbia, S.C., April 17, 1983, at 1-G.
2. Id.

The remedies available under the section will also be discussed.

This article will first trace the history of comparative advertising. The law's pre-Lanham Act approach to false and comparative advertising will be addressed next, with focus on *American Washboard Co. v. Saginaw Mfg. Co.*, its progeny, and the Trademark Act of 1920.

The next important change—the enactment of the Lanham Act in 1946—and the reasons for its passage will then be discussed briefly.

I. THE HISTORY OF COMPARATIVE ADVERTISING

A. Pre-1970

Commentators believe that Avis, in the mid-1960s, aired the first comparative ads. Although Avis never mentioned its competitor, the viewer knew Hertz was "Number 1" in the "We try harder" ads. S.O.S. soap pads used the next successful comparative ad campaign in its famous Big Blue versus Pink Pad advertisements.[3] These ads, although trail-blazers in the field of comparative advertising, demonstrate the era's general practice of comparing your product to a "Brand X."[4] Although the competitor was never mentioned, any knowledgeable viewer knew to whom the comparison was being made.

Various reasons explain the dearth of comparative ads prior to the late 1960s and early 1970s, including:

(1) Businesses considered mentioning a competitor a taboo because such a practice provided free publicity to the competitor by mentioning his/her product.[5] This is especially true for the market leaders, who gain very little by bringing attention to the competition.[6]

(2) Businesses feared that such "combative" techniques created sympathy for the product attacked.[7]

(3) Engaging in combative advertising was not considered gentlemanly. In essence, businesses thought the comparative ads were "unethical."[8]

(4) Businesses also feared the possibility of legal consequences stemming from such ads.[9]

---

3. Sterk, *The Law of Comparative Advertising: How Much Worse Is "Better" than "Great?"* 61 TRADE-MARK REP. 368, 369 (1977).
4. *Id.*
5. Sterk, *supra* note 3.
6. FORTUNE, February 13, 1978 at 104.
7. Sterk, *supra* note 3.
8. Hatry, *Comparative Advertising and a Recent Case Thereon,* 3 COM. & THE LAW 35, 38 (1981).
9. Sterk, *supra* note 3, at 368.

For these reasons, the three major television networks combined to create the biggest obstacle to comparative advertisements: the networks refused to air them.[10]

B. Post-1970: The Explosion

1. *The FTC Sees the Benefits of Comparative Advertising*

The restrictions on comparative advertising ended in the 1970s when the Federal Trade Commission (FTC) pressured the networks into accepting comparative ads because of their perceived "social value."[11] The FTC believed that ads showing the relative benefits and flaws of competing products better served the consuming public. They reasoned that if the competitor's product was "knocked," (s)he would fight back by improving the product or lowering the price.[12] Comparative ads, however, benefit the public only when accurate and truthful.

If an ad shows the relative flaws and benefits of two products, its value lies in providing the information for an intelligent purchasing decision. For example, Suave's ads claim that Suave products perform as well as leading brands, but at half the price. This ad benefits the consumer because, if the products perform equally and one is less expensive, the logical shopper purchases the less expensive product. If, however, the ad was false and the Suave product was not, in fact, the functional equivalent of the name brand, then the consumer relied on incorrect information in choosing a product. This causes the consumer to purchase an inferior product, expecting a product of quality equal to that of named brands. The ad "duped" the consumer into buying inferior merchandise.

Comparative ads also benefit advertisers, as they are one of the most informative (and most successful) types of advertising available.[13] Wendy's recent "Where's the Beef" ad campaign, in which Wendy's compares its "single" to McDonald's "Big Mac" and Burger King's "Whopper," increased Wendy's sales by twenty percent over a one-month span.[14]

Comparative ads can also lower market entry costs.[15] For example, when

---

10. Donegan, *Section 43(a) of the Lanham Act as a Private Remedy for False Advertising,* 37 Food Drug Cosm. L.J. 264 (1982).
11. Hatry, *supra* note 8, at 39.
12. Fortune, *supra* note 6, at 104.
13. The State, *supra* note 1, at 6-G.
14. The Washington Post, March 28, 1984, at B16, col. 1. The makers of Suave shampoo products increased their sales from $10 million to $50 million in four years after airing the comparative ads mentioned earlier. Fortune, *supra* note 6, at 111.
15. Thomson, *Problems of Proof in False Comparative Product Advertising: How Gullible is the Consumer?* 72 Trade-Mark Rep. 385, 387 (1982).

Savin broke into the office copying machine market, it did so by using comparative ads. Their television ads told secretaries that if they were sent to the Savin, they would find it "where the Xerox used to be." In newspapers, Savin's ads asked, "What do Xerox and IBM copiers have most in common?" The answer was: "Both are most commonly replaced by the Savin 780." This hugely successful ad campaign quadrupled Savin's sales.[16]

2. *The Networks Concede*

As mentioned earlier, in the mid-1970s, the FTC encouraged the networks to air comparative ads. The National Broadcasting Company (NBC) reacted first to the FTC's pressure in 1971 by broadcasting comparative advertisements.[17] The network established guidelines governing the use and format of comparative advertisements, including:

1. The products identified in the advertising must actually be in competition with one another.
2. Competitors shall be fairly and properly identified.
3. Advertisers shall refrain from discrediting, disparaging or unfairly attacking competitors, competing products or other industries.
4. The identification must be for comparison purposes and not simply to upgrade by association.
5. The advertising should compare related or similar properties or ingredients of the product, dimension to dimension, feature to feature, or wherever possible, by a side-by-side demonstration.
6. The property being compared must be significant in terms of value or usefulness of the product to the consumer.
7. The difference in properties must be measurable and significant.[18]

The other networks responded quickly, adopting similar guidelines.[19] The FTC also made a policy statement about comparative ads:

> Commission policy in the area of comparative advertising encourages the naming of, or reference to competitors, but requires clarity, and, if necessary, disclosure to avoid deception of the consumer. Additionally, the use of truthful comparative advertising should not be restrained by broadcasters or self-regulation entities.[20]

---

16. FORTUNE, *supra* note 6, at 111.
17. Conlon, *Comparative Advertising: Whatever Happened to "Brand X?"* 57 CHI. BAR RECORD 118 (1975); Hatry, *supra* note 8, at 38.
18. TRADE REG. REP, Current Comment 1969-1983, at 55,367.
19. Sterk, *supra* note 3, at 369.
20. 16 C.F.R. §14.15 (1980); Hatry, *supra* note 8, at 39.

3. *Comparative Advertising Overview*

All advertising rests somewhere on a continuum ranging from the clearly comparative to the exclusively noncomparative,[21] including, essentially, three types of comparative ads.

The most obvious type explicitly mentions the competitor and/or his/her product.[22] Within this category there are two subcategories: ads merely comparing "our" product to "their" product, and ads comparing "our" product to "their" product by "putting down" their product. The first group includes Suave's claim that its shampoo is as good as five other brands' shampoos at half the price, and Seven-Up's ads boasting no caffeine but making no value judgment about those beverages containing caffeine. The second group, those "putting down" the competitor's product, includes: Vanish toilet bowl cleaner's ad claiming the other brand wrecks plumbing; Scope mouthwash's advertisements referring to Listerine as giving "medicine breath"; Minute Maid lemonade's ad calling Country Time the "no lemon lemonade"; Totino's pizza's ads stating that other companies' pizzas have crusts tasting like "cardboard"; and another pizza marketer's ads claiming that its rival makes its cheese from "the main ingredient in some glues."[23]

The second type of comparative ad, almost as comparative as the first type, "readily identifies" the competitor.[24] This group includes the Avis and S.O.S. ads mentioned earlier.

The third type provides for consumer comparisons without identifying competitors, such as the comparison between "our brand" and "Brand X." These ads become more comparative when there are few competitors in the market.[25] For example, Jartran's comparative advertisements do not mention U-Haul, but U-Haul is, essentially, the only competitor.

II. PRE-LANHAM ACT APPROACH TO ADVERTISING

A. Common Law Actions

Victims of false advertising at common law had but two possible remedies: state law disparagement and false advertising actions. Litigants experienced many difficulties in these actions.[26] Additionally, before the Lanham Act, federal courts recognized no "property right" in a product which could be

21. Sterk, *supra* note 3, at 369.
22. *Id.*
23. Wall Street Journal, March 11, 1982, at 29, col. 1.
24. Sterk, *supra* note 3, at 369.
25. *Id.* at 370.
26. *Id.* at 378.

violated by false representations.[27]

One common law false advertising action was the "passing off" or "palming off" action. Palming off involves an attempt by one company to induce customers into believing that its product is actually that of its competitor.[28] The other action was the "misrepresentation of geographical origin" action. Some geographic areas become famous for quality products in a particular market (*e.g.*, furniture in Grand Rapids, sportswear in California, oranges in Florida). Regional businesses, in an effort to protect that reputation, attempt to prevent others from improperly labelling their goods as being from the favored area.[29] Some label this a subcategory of "passing off." If a manufacturer located in Newark calls itself the "Miami Orange Juice Co.," it merely passes its product off as a product of the named area.

Before granting relief, courts required that plaintiff prove direct economic injury.[30] Difficulties stemmed from the courts' requirement that plaintiff prove either: (1) the exact customers that were lost due to the defendant's acts; or (2) that defendant's acts directly caused plaintiff's lost sales. The problem arose due to the courts' inability to determine, with precision, the number of sales defendant's representations caused plaintiff to lose. Although plaintiff often proved (s)he lost *some* business, courts rarely determined the number with sufficient accuracy for a finding of injury or potential injury.[31]

---

27. Derenberg, *Federal Unfair Competition Law at the End of the First Decade of the Lanham Act: Prologue or Epilogue?* 32 N.Y.U. L. REV. 1029, 1032. *See* American Washboard Co. v. Saginaw Mfg. Co., 103 F. 281 (6th Cir. 1900).
28. Donegan, *supra* note 10, at 268.
29. *See* Grand Rapids Furniture Co. v. Grand Rapids Furniture Co., 127 F.2d 245 (7th Cir. 1942). Misrepresentation of origin cases are not limited only to geographic origin. The category now includes misrepresentation of manufacturer as well. *See, e.g.,* Gage-Downs Co. v. Featherstone Corset Co., 83 F. 213 (C.C.W.D. Mich. 1897). There, the defendant advertised its corsets as "Chicage Waists." Plaintiff had long been associated with that name and sought an injunction. In granting plaintiff's relief, the court stated that,

> the circumstances vary greatly, but the underlying principle which is effective in the solution of such cases is that a party may not adopt a mark or symbol which has been employed by another manufacturer, and by long use and employment on the part of that other has come to be recognized by the public as denoting the origin of manufacture, and thus impose upon the public by inducing them to believe that the goods which the new party thus offers are the goods of the original party.

83 F. at 213. *See also* Federal-Mogul-Bower Bearing, Inc. v. Azoff, 313 F.2d 405 (6th Cir. 1963).
30. *Id.*
31. Donegan, *supra* note 10, at 269. *See also* Gold Seal Co. v. Weeks, 129 F. Supp. 928 (D.D.C. 1955).

1. *Disparagement and Defamation*

At common law, advertisers making false statements about a competitor's product were liable under the rules of defamation and disparagement.[32] Defamation is defined as "a communication which tends to damage the plaintiff's 'reputation' more or less in the popular sense—that is, to diminish the respect, good will, confidence or esteem in which he is held, or to excite adverse or unpleasant feeling about him."[33] Disparagement is "a deliberate, demonstrably false attack upon plaintiff's product."[34] The applicable rule, although slightly different in different states, said "[D]isparagement exists if the quality of plaintiff's goods or products is impugned, while an attack on plaintiff's honesty or integrity phrased as an insult to the goods brings on a cause of action for defamation."[35]

To succeed in a disparagement action, plaintiff "must show either 'scienter' that the statement published is false, or an intent to do harm to the plaintiff, or to affect his interests adversely in an unprivileged manner."[36] In addition, plaintiff must prove the statement's falsity.[37] Disparagement actions require that plaintiff show special damages, which greatly decreases the chance of success. Even the most liberal courts require proof "(1) of lost profits, (2) proximately caused by defendant's wrongful act."[38]

Finally, disparagement actions provided money damages, not injunctive relief.[39] Courts assumed that injunctions restricted free speech,[40] "[e]ven if control of advertising is permitted, however, there may be constitutional limits on the relief which can be provided. In theory, allowing injuctions to issue poses a potentially greater threat to free speech than does the awared of damages to a competitor."[41] The Supreme Court's recent decisions, however, alter this stance, stating the "the interest in protecting the public and competitors from deceptive comparative advertising will usually outweigh any First Amendment interests in this area."[42]

---

32. This was often defined as "trade libel" or "injurious falsehood." Sterk, *supra* note 3, at 370.
33. *Id.*
34. *Id.*
35. *Id.*
36. *Id.* at 372.
37. *Id.*
38. *Id.,* quoting Dale System, Inc. v. Time, Inc., 116 F. Supp. 527, 535 (D. Conn. 1953).
39. *Id.* at 374.
40. *Id.*
41. *Id.* The Constitutional implications of enjoining false or comparative ads are beyond the scope of this article. To explore the constitutional issues, read: *Developments in the Law—Competitive Torts,* 77 HARV. L. REV. 888 (1964); Note, Freedom of Expression in a Commercial Context, 78 HARV. L. REV. 1191 (1965); 1 G. ROSDEN AND P. ROSDEN, THE LAW OF ADVERTISING, §6.01–6.04 (1973–74).
42. *Id.* at 374 n. 27.

2. *Unfair Competition*

American Washboard Co. v. Saginaw Mfg. Co. governed unfair competition actions at common law. This case, often criticized as applying the controlling law of the time too narrowly, precluded any possible recovery for false advertising.[43]

American Washboard manufactured the only washboard with an all-aluminum face. Saginaw, a competitor, marketed a washboard with a zinc face advertised as aluminum. The court denied American Washboard's relief, stating that its claim

> loses sight of the thoroughly established principle that the private right of action in such cases [palming off] is not based upon fraud or imposition upon the public, but is maintained solely for the protection of property right of the complainant . . . it is only where [the] deception induces the public to buy the goods as those of complainant that a private right of action arises.[44]

American Washboard remained the standard, forcing all unfair competition protection into the exclusive domain of the FTC.[45] Part of the problem in this area, mentioned earlier, flowed from the courts' inability to determine accurately plaintiff's lost sales. Plaintiff prevailed if (s)he proved the number of lost sales. *Ely-Norris Safe Co. v. Mosler Safe Co.* (7 F.2d 603 (2d Cir. 1925)) demonstrates the standard for recovery. Ely-Norris held the patent on safes with explosion chambers. Mosler misrepresented that its safes also had such a feature. Judge Learned Hand, in an oft-quoted passage, said that "there is no part of the law that is more plastic than unfair competition, and what was not reckoned an actionable wrong twenty-five years ago may have become such today."[46] Ely-Norris recovered because it showed that, as patent holder, it lost sales. Although the court's language indicated a slight movement away from the restrictive language of the *American Washboard* case, no such trend developed and the narrow common law rule prevailed.

Nuisance law, which allows an individual to recover for a public nuisance only if his/her injury differs in kind from the injury suffered by the general

---

43. HANDLER, FALSE AND MISLEADING ADVERTISING, 39 YALE L. J. 22 (1929); Derenberg, *supra* note 27, at 1032.
44. American Washboard Co. v. Saginaw Mfg. Co., 103 F. 281, 285 (6th Cir. 1900).
45. Derenberg, *supra* note 27, at 1032.
46. As is usually the case, Learned Hand proved to be ahead of his time with this statement, which is quoted in virtually every article and decision dealing with Section 43(a).

public,[47] contributed to the common law rule.

Foreign producers, desiring more protection in the American market than the common law provided, began voicing their displeasure to Congress.[48] Congress realized as far back as 1924 that the United States should follow the practice established in certain foreign countries. In those countries, an injured competitor could bring a civil suit, even in the absence of any specific property right, when a competitor made a false designation of origin or false description.[49]

B. The Trademark Act of 1920

The Trademark Act of 1920 represents Congress' first attempt at remedying the problem. That Act implemented the provisions of certain treaties granting protection to foreign concerns for possible misrepresentations by American companies (*e.g.*, the Buenos Aires Convention of 1910).

Section (3) of the Trademark Act of 1920 "for the first time, provided a federal statutory basis for private protection against one particular type of unfair competition not resulting from the infringement of a registered trademark."[50] Courts construed the section very narrowly, causing plaintiffs to use it rarely. The section was impotent because: (1) it excluded forms of misrepresentation and applied only to false designations of origin; (2) it applied to merchandise, but not to services; and (3) it required the plaintiff to show that the party responsible for the ad willfully and intentionally used false advertising with an intent to deceive.[51] These requirements rendered the Act practically useless.[52]

III. THE LANHAM ACT

As a reaction to the inadequacies of the common law and the Trademark Act of 1920, Congress passed the Lanham Act in 1946.[53]

A. Section 43(a)

Section 43(a) of the Lanham Act, 15 U.S.C. Section 1125(a), covers com-

---

47. Derenberg, *supra* note 27, at 1033.
48. Donegan, *supra* note 10, at 271.
49. Marx, 40 WASH. & LEE L. REV. 383, 389–90. *See also* Derenberg, *supra* note 27, at 1034.
50. *See* Derenberg, *supra* note 27, at 1034.
51. *Id.*
52. "Almost no reported decision can be found in which relief was granted . . . based on this newly created remedy." Derenberg, *supra* note 27, at 1034.
53. Bunn, *The National Law of Unfair Competition,* 62 HARV. L. REV. 987, 998–1000 (1949).

parative advertising. That section provides, in pertinent part:

> Any person who shall . . . use in connection with any goods
> . . . any false description or representation, including words
> or other symbols tending falsely to describe or represent the
> same, and shall cause such goods or services to enter into com-
> merce, . . . shall be liable to a civil action by . . . any person
> who believes that he is or is likely to be damaged by the use
> of any such false description or representation.[54]

Courts refused, however, to expand the scope of advertising law with less
than thirty reported cases under section 43(a) by 1964.[55] Now, however, section 43(a) is one of the most litigated federal statutes.[56]

Originally, courts treated section 43(a) as a codification of the common
law, consequently reducing both the number of actions brought under the section and the frequency of recovery. This approach continued until the Third
Circuit Court of Appeals decision in *L'Aiglon Apparel, Inc. v. Lana Lobel
Inc.* L'Aiglon, the plaintiff, sold a distinctive dress for $17.95 using a large
ad campaign. Lana Lobel sold a different dress of inferior quality. Lobel's
ads pictured one of L'Aiglon's dresses with Lobel's name and a price of $6.95.
The misleading nature of Lobel's ads provoked L'Aiglon's suit. The court stated
that section 43(a) eliminated the common law rules of the *American Washboard*
case.[57] The court indicated that nothing in the Act's legislative history implied the codification of the common law and, therefore, plaintiff stated a
valid cause of action.[58] The court continued: "[H]ere is a provision of a federal
statute which, with clarity and precision adequate for judicial administration,
creates and defines rights and duties and provides for their vindication in the
federal courts."[59] One court held that the enactment of section 43(a) "marked

54. "The term 'false' has been construed to include those claims which are misleading
or deceptive, as well as those which are literally untrue." Thomas J. Donegan, *Section 43(a) of the Lanham Act as a Private Remedy for False Advertising,* 37 FOOD
DRUG COSM. L. REP. 264, 265 (1982).
55. As of 1964, plaintiffs invoked Section 43(a) in less than thirty cases. *See* Note,
Developments in the Law—Competitive Torts, 77 HARV. L. REV. 888, 908 (1964). For
a case involving a narrow interpretation of Section 43(a), thereby stifling the section's usefulness, *see* Samson Crane Co. v. Union National Sales, 87 F. Supp. 218
(D. Mass. 1949), *aff'd* 180 F.2d 896 (1st Cir. 1950), in which the court stated that
Section 43(a) ". . . should not be interpreted so as to bring within its scope any kind
of undesirable business practice which involves deception . . . especially when
such . . . practices are already the subject of other Congressional legislation, such
as the Federal Trade Commission Act." 87 F. Supp. at 222.
56. Lee, *Comparative Advertising, Commercial Disparagement and False Advertising,*
71 TRADE-MARK REP. 620, 629 (1981).
57. L'Aiglon Apparel, Inc. v. Lana Lobel Inc., 214 F.2d 649, 651 (3d Cir. 1954).
58. *Id.*
59. *Id.*

the creation of a 'new statutory tort' intended to secure a marketplace free from deceitful marketing practices."[60] Another court held that section 43(a) created a federal statutory tort, *"sui generis."*[61]

The increase in actions under section 43(a) has resulted from: (1) the FTC's decision to decrease its activity in the field; (2) the present administration's attitude; and (3) the red tape, expense and time necessary for FTC actions.[62] Consequently, the industry, through private litigation, developed a self-policing policy.[63]

The drastic change in the advertising market since the Lanham Act's passage helped spark the recent increase in litigation under section 43(a). As television developed into the most "pervasive force in American society," businesses increased their advertising.[64] Television reaches millions of people, offering advertisers an opportunity for exposure not available in other mediums.[65] Comparative advertising increased with the popularity of television,[66] which increased the number of actions filed under section 43(a).[67]

B. Actions Under Section 43(a)

When aggrieved by an ad, most companies protest first to the networks themselves, hoping the ad will be recalled. In 1981, the American Broadcasting Company (ABC) received 131 such complaints and upheld thirty percent of them.[68] If the network does not comply, the next step is the National Advertising Division of the Council of Better Business Bureaus (N.A.D.). The N.A.D. acts as an appellate review board for competitors with grievances.[69] If that fails, section 43(a) may be used in private litigation.

1. *Jurisdiction Under Section 43(a)*

Courts generally interpret section 43(a)'s jurisdiction broadly. Section

---

60. Johnson & Johnson v. Carter-Wallace, Inc., 631 F.2d 186, 189 (2d Cir. 1980), *citing* L'Aiglon, 214 F.2d 649, 651 (3d Cir. 1954).
61. Gold Seal v. Weeks, 129 F. Supp. 928 (D. D.C. 1955).
62. "The Chairman of the FTC . . . has recently expressed his interest to encourage the FTC not to regulate activity in this area . . . [unless the ads] pose a threat of significant injury to the public that cannot be cured by market forces." Marx, *supra* note 49, at 385.
63. Donegan, *supra* note 10.
64. Donegan, *supra* note 10, at 265. Advertising expenditures are estimated at $85.4 billion for 1984. In addition, the cost of a thirty-second ad has quadrupled since 1973. *See* NEWSWEEK, March 26, 1984, at 62.
65. Donegan, *supra* note 10, at 265.
66. *See* text accompanying *supra* note 2.
67. Donegan, *supra* note 10, at 264; Lee, *supra* note 56, at 629.
68. Wall Street Journal, March 11, 1982, at 29, col. 1.
69. Hatry, *supra* note 8, at 39.

39 of the Lanham Act grants federal courts jurisdiction over "all actions arising under this act, without regard to the amount in controversy or to diversity or lack of diversity of the citizenship of the parties." Most courts maintain section 39 jurisdiction even though the plaintiff lacks a federally registered trademark.[70] Courts do, however, require that common law trademarks have a "secondary meaning."[71]

Jurisdiction can be found outside section 39 as well. Section 1338(a) of the Judicial Code also gives federal district courts jurisdiction over section 43(a) actions. That section provides that the federal courts have "original jurisdiction of any civil action arising under any Act of Congress relating to patents, plant variety protection, copyrights and trademarks."[72]

2. *Standing to Sue*

a. *The Language of the Act*

Section 43(a) gives two classes of "persons" standing to sue: (1) any person doing business in the locality falsely indicated as that of origin or in the region in which said locality is situated; and (2) any person who believes that (s)he is or is likely to be damaged by the use of any such false description or representation.[73]

The first group reflects the pre-Lanham Act actions for false designation of geographic origin,[74] supporting the contention that section 43(a) supplants common law actions for false designation of origin. The second group provides even more strength to that contention. That group includes "any person who believes that he is or is likely to be damaged." That broad language appears to give standing to a large number of potential plaintiffs. Courts,

---

70. *See* General Pool Corp. v. Hallmark Pool Corp., 259 F. Supp. 383 (N.D. Ill. 1966).
71. Germain, *Unfair Trade Practices Under Section 43(a) of the Lanham Act: You've Come a Long Way, Baby—Too Far Maybe?* 49 IND. L.J. 84, 92 (1973).

> Secondary meaning traditionally applies to a work which is originally descriptive: It contemplates that a word or phrase originally, and in that sense primarily, incapable of exclusive appropriation with reference to an article on the market, because. . .descriptive, might nevertheless have been used so long and so exclusively by one producer with reference to his article that. . .the work or phrase had come to mean that the article was his product.

> Comment, *The Present Scope of Recovery for Unfair Competition Violation Under Section 43(a) of the Lanham Act,* 58 NEBR. L. R. 159, 165 n. 49, *quoting* G. & C. Merriam Co. v. Saalfield, 198 F. 369, 373 (6th Cir. 1912).

72. 28 U.S.C. §1338(a) (Vol. 8 1976). *See, e.g.,* Bose Corp. v. Linear Design Labs, Inc., 340 F. Supp. 513 (S.D.N.Y. 1971).
73. Germain, *supra* note 71, at 92.
74. *Id.*

however, prevent standing from greatly expanding by limiting the statute's broad language. They achieve the limitation by requiring that only parties in direct competition have standing.

b. *The Direct Competition Requirement*

Upon enactment of the statute, the FTC protected consumers, diminishing the importance of the direct competition requirement. Only competitors needed section 43(a) protection. The FTC's recent trend away from consumer protection should lead to a re-evaluation of section 43(a)'s standing requirements.[75]

Trade Associations. The demise of the direct competition requirement began in the 1959 case *Mutation Mink Breeders Association v. Lou Nierenberg, Corp.* Mutation Mink, a trade organization with greater then 5,000 members throughout the U.S., sued Nierenberg, a fabric finishing company marketing imitation mink products called "Normink."[76] Mutation Mink claimed Nierenberg falsely represented its product as genuine mink and sought an injunction, damages, and an accounting of profits.

The court discussed the common law "single source" rule, which denied a plaintiff recovery in a palming-off action unless (s)he could show that the origin was from a single, though anonymous, source. At common law, if the plaintiff failed to prove which party would be injured, (s)he recovered nothing.[77]

The court rejected Nierenberg's claim that the single source rule barred recovery, stating "the 'single source' rule is inapplicable to suits under section 43(a) and that the 'likely to be damaged' provision of section 43(a) obviates the necessity of proving actual diversion of trade."[78] The court reaffirmed the position that "Section 43(a) of the Lanham Act creates a new 'federal statutory tort, *sui generis'* and does not merely codify the common law principles of unfair competition."[79]

Nierenberg further claimed that Mutation Mink lacked standing because it had no pecuniary interest in the market. The court, however, held that plaintiff did have a pecuniary interest because "in return for its services to its members it receives a percentage of the sales price of the pelts sold by them."[80]

Although *Mutation Mink* marked a step toward broadened standing under section 43(a), one could argue that the trade organization had no identity apart

---

75. This trend continues and it does not appear that there will be any changes in policy in the near future. *See* The Washington Post, March 24, 1984, at D17.
76. Mutation Mink Breeders Association v. Lou Nierenberg, Corp., 23 F.R.D. 155, 158 (S.D.N.Y. 1959).
77. *See* Mosler Safe Co. v. Ely-Norris Safe Co., 273 U.S. 132 (1927); American Washboard Co. v. Saginaw Mfg. Co., 103 F. 281 (6th Cir. 1900).
78. Mutation Mink Breeders Association v. Lou Nierenberg, Corp., 23 F.R.D. 155, 161 (S.D.N.Y. 1959). *See also,* Gold Seal v. Weeks, 129 F. Supp. 928 (D. D.C. 1955).
79. *Id.* at 161, *quoting* Gold Seal, 129 F. Supp. 928, 940 (D. D.C. 1955).
80. *Id.* at 162.

from its members. Therefore, the organization was, in fact, in direct competition with defendant since its income, based on pelt sales, obviously decreased as a result of defendant's practices.

Florida v. Real Juices, Inc. also broadened standing under section 43(a). Plaintiff, the Florida Department of Citrus, claimed that Real Juices, a corporation marketing an orange juice under the name "Sunshine Tree,"[81] infringed upon Florida's unregistered certification mark.[82] Florida's mark identified citrus products originating in Florida.

The court first held that section 43(a) protected Florida's common law certification mark.[83] The court stated further that any "proprietary right" to "Sunshine Tree"'s good will belonged to Florida, which could associate the slogan with any products it desired.[84] By selling its product under the same name, Real Juices implied an affiliation with plaintiff's advertising. The court determined that any opinions formed about defendant's product affected opinions of products associated with the mark "Sunshine Tree," defeating Florida's desire to establish the mark as a symbol of quality, origin, and source. The court granted an injunction because of the likelihood of Florida suffering irreparable injury.[85] The court allowed Florida's suit even though the state did not compete with the defendant and lacked a direct pecuniary interest in defendant's business.

Some commentators argue that Florida had an interest in the good will of the "Sunshine Tree."[86] One might be persuaded that Florida's pecuniary interest lay in the revenue obtained through taxes, jobs, and other benefits of the citrus business. If defendant's practices marred the citrus industry's reputation in some way or affected the industry's good will, Florida could claim direct injury as a result of a decline in the citrus industry.

Consumer Standing. In 1971, some important cases shed light on the consumer standing issue, still a controversial and unsettled area in section 43(a) litigation.

In *Arneson v. Raymond Lee Organization,* the court permitted a consumer to bring an action under section 43(a). Arneson, an inventor bringing a class action on behalf of himself and all other inventors similarly situated, claimed the defendant, a patent service, lured clients through misleading advertisements. The court reasoned that "the liability of Section 43(a) is clear on its face, it applies to any person who is or is likely to be damaged. . . . The

---

81. Florida v. Real Juices, Inc., 330 F. Supp. 428, 429 (M.D. Fla. 1971).
82. The reader may recall Anita Bryant singing the praises of the "Florida Sunshine Tree" in various television and radio ads.
83. Florida v. Real Juices, Inc., 330 F. Supp. 428, 430 (M.D. Fla. 1971).
84. *Id.* at 432.
85. *Id.* at 434.
86. *See* Germain, *supra* note 71, at 93.

plain language of the intent section [Section 45] makes actionable, *inter alia,* the deceptive and misleading use of marks and descriptions."[87]

Conversely, the Second Circuit, a perennial leader in trademark actions, in *Colligan v. Activities Club of New York, Ltd.,* denied standing to two students, as consumers, in their action against a ski tour service alleging misrepresentations about their tour service. That court provided a thorough analysis for its decision.[88]

Initially, the court noted that the plain language of section 43(a) seemed to support the plaintiffs' contention that they had standing to sue:

> On the face of the complaint all the prerequisites of Section 43(a) seem to be met: (1)defendants are persons (2) who used false descriptions and misrepresentations (3) in connection with goods and services (4) which defendant caused to enter commerce; (5) appellants are also persons (6) who believe themselves to have been in fact damaged by defendant's misdescriptions and misrepresentation.

The court, however, refused to look at the statute in a vacuum and quoted Learned Hand:"[W]ords are not pebbles in alien juxtaposition," and analyzed the section accordingly.[89]

The court also ignored the Act's legislative history; it stated that, "the legislative history of the Act, such as it is, adds nothing"[90] and then focused on section 45 of the Act—the "intent" section. The court relied heavily on that section's language which provides, in pertinent part: "The intent of this chapter . . . is to protect persons engaged in such commerce against unfair competition."[91] The court found the absence of any reference to "public" or "consumers" determinative of the issue, concluding that "Congress' purpose in enacting section 43(a) was to create a special and limited unfair competition remedy, virtually without regard for the interests of consumers generally and almost certainly without any consideration of consumer rights of action in particular."[92]

---

87. Arneson v. Raymond Lee Organization, 333 F. Supp. 116, 120 (C.D. Cal. 1971). *See also* Yameta v. Capitol Records, Inc., 279 F. Supp. 582 (S.D.N.Y. 1968).
88. One could discern, however, from the very beginning of the opinion that the plaintiffs would meet an unhappy fate when the judge, referring to plaintiff's cause of action, said that "appellants *imaginatively* have brought this action pursuant to [sections] 39 and 43(a) of the Lanham Act." Colligan v. Activities Club of New York, Ltd., 442 F.2d 686, 688 (2d Cir. 1971).
89. *Id.* at 689, *quoting* NLRB v. Federbush Co., Inc., 121 F.2d 954, 957 (2d Cir. 1941).
90. *Id.* at 691.
91. 15 U.S.C. §1127 (West 1982).
92. Colligan v. Activities Club of New York, Ltd., 442 F.2d 686, 692 (2d Cir. 1971).

A. ANDREW GALLO

The court mentioned, however, that an expansive reading "would lead to a veritable flood of claims brought in already overtaxed federal district courts. . . ."[93] The author contends that the court relied upon the latter reason most heavily.

The court ignored plaintiff's analysis of the Act's legislative history and plain language. First, the court ignored the statute's "plain meaning" as submitted by the plaintiff. Section 43(a) provides, unambiguously, that "*any person* who believes that *he* is or is likely to be damaged" (emphasis added) may bring a civil action. The *Arneson* court interpreted the clear language as reflecting Congress' intent to permit consumer actions under the Act.

A United States Trademark Association representative offered one of many compelling reasons for interpreting standing broadly when he spoke to a joint congressional committee in 1925. The committee investigated a bill which, basically, became section 43(a). The Trademark Association representative stated:

> The section provides that any person who is damaged by the false description may start the suit. Obviously, the purchaser might claim that he has been misled and damaged and start suit. At any rate, if it is intended to limit the right to start such a suit, that limitation should be stated.[94]

After this statement, the provision remained unchanged, evidencing the committee's intent to provide protection to consumers.[95]

Additional reasons exist for providing standing to consumers under the Act. As mentioned earlier, [96] section 3 of the Trademark Act of 1920 preceded section 43(a). That section applied only to persons, corporations, etc. "doing business" in the falsely indicated locality. Congress employed the same language in some of the tentative drafts of section 43(a).[97] The version finally enacted, however, contains no such limiting language. The absence of such

---

93. *Id.* at 693.
94. *Id.* at 690, *quoting* Joint Hearings Before the Committee on Patents, 68th Cong., 2d Sess. 127–128 (1925) (statement of Arthur W. Barber).
95. 2A C. DALLAS SANDS, STATUTES AND STATUTORY CONSTRUCTION, §48.10 (1973) at 209. The court in *Colligan* referred to this as a "flimsy record" and chose to interpret the committee's inaction as merely indicating that the committee did not think the statement deserved a response. Colligan v. Activities Club of New York, Ltd., 686, 690 (2d Cir. 1971).
96. *See* text accompanying *supra* notes 50–52.
97. *E.g.,* one version provided a cause of action to "any person. . .who is or is likely to be *damaged in his trade or business* by any false description. . . ." (emphasis supplied) Colligan v. Activities Club of New York, Ltd., 442 F.2d 686, 691 (2d Cir. 1971), *quoting* Misc. Bar Ass'n Reps., v. 22, item 26, section 27, Ass'n of the Bar of N.Y. catal. no. BA Misc. 681, v. 22.

limiting language is important in construing Congress' intent.[98] If Congress intended to limit section 43(a) to actions brought by competitors or those with commercial interests only, it could easily have included such language in the section.[99]

The recent government trend away from consumer protection provides the final, and perhaps most persuasive, reason for protecting consumers under section 43(a). As the court in *Colligan* stated, Congress did not foresee the "consumer protection explosion and the wholesale displacement . . . of traditional state authority and common law remedies. . . ."[100] Even so, the *Colligan* court believed that the FTC protected the rights of consumers and seemed uninterested in consumer protection. That court stated, in a footnote: "Although we hold that consumers have no right of action under Section 43(a), we note that the federal government through the FTC has intervened in the marketplace and in the courts to vindicate the rights of the consuming public."[101] The court quoted Chief Judge Clark in *California Apparel Creators v. Wieder of California,* where he said: "So far as the consumer is concerned, he is not dependant upon the private remedial actions brought by competitors for the remedies under the Federal Trade Commission Act . . . are now extensive. . . ."[102]

Although appropriate in 1947 and, perhaps, even in 1971, a re-evaluation of such an approach is necessary, due to the FTC's questionable track record coupled with its recent decision to decrease its role in the area of consumer protection.[103] That decision occured in the mid-1970s[104] and, therefore, did not affect the *Colligan* court's decision.

Consumers, the group most likely to be injured by a false or misleading comparative ad, must have a remedy. If an ad purportedly compares two products' relative flaws and benefits and does not convey truthful, clear statements, then consumers will be relying on incorrect information when making their purchase choices. Consequently, consumers will purchase goods differing from their expectation. In *Colligan,* the defendant's ads about its ski service injured a group of consumers. No competitor was injured and, therefore, no one else brought an action against the tour company to enjoin its misleading

---

98. Sands, *supra* note 95, § 48.03, at 191.
99. Sands, *supra* note 95, § 47.37, at 167. *See also* Colligan v. Activities Club of New York, Ltd., 442 F.2d 686, 693 (2d Cir. 1971). Regardless of the foregoing, the court chose to use the opposite interpretation: "[H]ad Congress contemplated so revolutionary a departure implicit in appellants' claims, its intention could and would have been clearly expressed." Colligan v. Activities Club of New York, Ltd., 442 F.2d 686, 694 (2d Cir. 1971).
100. Colligan v. Activities Club of New York, Ltd., 442 F.2d 686, 691 (2d Cir. 1971).
101. *Id.* at 694 n.37.
102. California Apparel Creators v. Wieder of California, 162 F.2d 893, 896 (2d Cir. 1947).
103. *See* The Washington Post, March 24, 1984, at D17. *See also,* Baum, *The Consumer and the Federal Trade Commission,* 44 J. URB. L. 71 (1966); Donegan, *supra* note 10.
104. *Id., supra* note 10.

ads. Consequently, only common law remedies, under which recovery is difficult, remain. As a result of being in state courts, consumers also are deprived of the federal court system's benefits.

Plaintiffs in these cases prefer federal courts. First, plaintiffs face great difficulties in bringing class actions in state courts. More importantly, state common law claims impair recovery. Federal courts also offer procedural advantages not available in state courts.

Additionally, federal courts impose more efficient and effective remedies. Injunctions, less available under state law, maintain effectiveness only within the boundaries of that state. An injunction issued by a federal court controls in all states. Finally, consumers anticipate greater success given a federal statutory remedy because section 43(a) makes recovery easier than common law rules.

3. Remedies

a. Injunctions

Plaintiffs most often pursue injunctions seeking retraction of their competitor's advertisement. For an injunction to issue, plaintiff must show:
   (1) likelihood of success on the merits;
   (2) that it has suffered, and is likely to continue to suffer, irreparable injury to its market share or the good will of its product; and
   (3) that the balance of equities tips decidedly in favor of granting preliminary relief.[105]

The Lanham Act lowers the irreparable injury standard.[106] Plaintiff must prove a *reasonable* basis to believe that the false advertising will result in damage. To obtain an injunction, plaintiff need only show the ad's *tendency* to deceive.[107]

Some courts *presume* irreparable harm.[108] In *Philip Morris v. Loew's Theatres, Inc.* Philip Moris challenged Loew's comparative ads in which Loew's claimed that smokers preferred Triumph cigarettes over Merit.[109] Philip Morris sought an injunction attacking the methodology of defendant's taste test. In granting the injunction, the court stated that, "Brand loyalty would be affected and by its very nature would remain incalculable . . . and the reputation of plaintiff, a direct competitor, among consumers will thereby

---

105. Thomson, *supra* note 15, at 391.
106. Johnson & Johnson v. Carter-Wallace, Inc., 631 F.2d 186 (2d Cir. 1980).
107. American Brands v. R. J. Reynolds Tobacco Co., 413 F. Supp. 1352, 1356 (S.D.N.Y. 1976).
108. Quaker State Oil Refining Corp. v. Burmah-Castrol, Inc., 504 F. Supp. 178, 182 (S.D.N.Y. 1980).
109. Philip Morris v. Loew's Theatres, Inc., 511 F. Supp. 855, 857 (S.D.N.Y. 1980).

suffer."[110]

In *McNeilab v. American Home Products Corp.*,[111] the court stated that the plaintiff need not show *actual* injury to obtain injunctive relief. McNeilab produced Extra-Strength Tylenol (EST) and American Home Products produced Maximum Strength Anacin (MSA). McNeilab sought to enjoin American Home Products from airing certain ads which, although literally true, implied Anacin's superiority over Tylenol when, in fact, both products contained the same amount of pain reliever.[112] The court held that plaintiff must show only the *potential for injury:* "Continued airing would appear to threaten injury since it is difficult to believe that, over the long run, continued claims of competitive superiority would not eventually detract from a competitor's sales and goodwill."[113]

Courts recognize the public policies involved: "[I]t is the public interest as well as the competitor which is to be protected from deceptive advertising, and only injunctive relief can prevent that irreparable injury."[114]

Finally, because an injuction constitutes an equitable remedy, plaintiffs must enter court with "clean hands." In *Haagen Daz v. Frusen Gladje* (493 F. Supp. 73 (S.D.N.Y. 1980), for example, Haagen Daz sought to enjoin Frusen Gladje from confusing the public by implying that its product was made in Sweden. The court denied the relief, stating that it would not aid Haagen Daz because it engaged in the same practice.[115]

b. *Damages*

Although often sought, courts rarely award damages. To obtain damages, plaintiff must successfully prove actual consumer reliance on the advertisement.[116] Plaintiff must also show a causal realtionship between the ad in question and a loss of business: "[P]laintiff must show a nexus between the alleged violation and the injuries suffered."[117]

C. Elements of a Cause of Action Under Section 43(a)

An action under section 43(a) must contain these elements:
(1) In its comparative advertisement, the defendant must make false statements of fact about its own product;

---

110. *Id.* at 858.
111. McNeilab v. American Home Products Corp., 501 F. Supp. 517 (S.D.N.Y. 1980).
112. *Id.* at 521.
113. *Id.* at 539.
114. Philip Morris v. Loew's Theatres, Inc., 511 F. Supp. 855, 858 (S.D.N.Y. 1980).
115. One could argue that the court's decision harmed only the consumer. The old saying, "two wrongs don't make a right," seems more than appropriate in this case.
116. Skil Corp. v. Rockwell International Corp., 375 F. Supp. 777 (N.D. Ill. 1974); Toro Co. v. Textron, Inc., 499 F. Supp. 241, 251 (D. Del. 1980).
117. Thomson, *supra* note 15, at 399.

(2) Those advertisements must actually deceive or have a tendency to deceive a substantial segment of the audience;

(3) Such deception must be material, in that it is likely to influence a purchasing decision;

(4) Defendant's product must enter interstate commerce;[118] and

(5) Plaintiff must have been or be likely to be injured as the result of the foregoing by direct diversion of sales from itself to defendant, or by lessening of the goodwill which its products enjoy with the buying public.[119]

1. *False Statements about Defendant's Own Product*

The first requirement, that defendant make false statements of fact about its own product, causes some controversy. The general rule states that if a defendant merely makes claims about the plaintiff's product, no action will lie under section 43(a).[120] Some commentators, however, argue that false claims made about plaintiff's products should support a section 43(a) action because such assertions make *implicit* claims of superiority. [121]

Defendant's false statements about plaintiff's product should constitute actionable advertising. If defendant's false statements about plaintiff's product imply the inferiority of plantiff's product, unfair competition exists.[122] Section 43(a) was specifically enacted "to protect persons engaged in . . . commerce against unfair competition."[123] A narrow interpretation of the section's language flies in the face of other decisions holding that section 43(a) acts as a "remedial statute and should be broadly rather than strictly construed."[124]

In *Skil Corp. v. Rockwell International Corp.*, Skil alleged that Rockwell's ads made false and misleading factual statements and comparisons with Skil's products.[125] The court stated that

> it does not seem logical to distinguish between a false statement about the plaintiff's product and a false statement about

---

118. Commerce is defined in 15 U.S.C. as "all commerce which may be lawfully regulated by Congress." Failure to plead and prove that the product entered into commerce will lead to a dismissal. Iding v. Anaston, 266 F. Supp. 1015 (N.D. Ill. 1969).

119. Skil Corp. v. Rockwell International Corp., 375 F. Supp. 777, 783 (N.D. Ill. 1974); U-Haul International, Inc. v. Jartran, Inc., 522 F. Supp. 1238 (D. Ariz. 1981).

120. Bernard Food Industries v. Dietene, 415 F.2d 1279 (7th Cir. 1969); Ragold, Inc. v. Ferraro, U.S.A., 506 F. Supp. 117 (N.D. Ill. 1980).

121. Lee, *supra* note 56, at 631.

122. Note, *Section 43(a) of the Lanham Act: Its Development and Potential,* 3 LOY. L REV. 327, 337 (1972).

123. 15 U.S.C. Section 1127 (West 1982).

124. Midwest Packaging Materials Company v. Midwest Packaging Corp., 312 F. Supp. 134, 135 (S.D. Iowa 1970).

125. Skil Corp. v. Rockwe'' Internation; ' (rp., 375 F. Supp. 777, 779 (N.D. Ill. 1974).

> defendant's product in a case where the particular statement
> is contained in comparison advertising by the defendant, such
> that in the first instance the plaintiff does not have a cause of
> action whereas in the latter he does. . . . Rather, it would
> seem that in comparison advertising, a false statement by the
> defendant about plaintiff's product would have the same
> detrimental effect as a false statement about defendant's pro-
> duct. I.e., it would tend to mislead the buying public concern-
> ing the relative merits and qualities of the products, thereby
> inducing the purchase of a possibly inferior product. . . .[126]

The court argues persuasively, especially in light of the fact that comparative ads give an impression about *both* products and their relation to one another.

However, the general rule instructs that if the defendant makes statements only about plaintiff's product, plaintiff must rely on the common law of disparagement for relief.

2. *Deception or Tendency to Deceive*

The second requirement, that the ad actually deceive or tend to deceive a substantial segment of the audience, causes the most controversy in section 43(a) cases.

a. *Facial Falsity*

As mentioned earlier, the Trademark Act of 1920 failed because it re-
quired plaintiffs to prove that defendant willfully or intentionally made false representations.[127] Section 43(a) contains no such requirement.[128] Plaintiff need not show that defendant *intended* public deception. The court, first and most importantly, must ask whether the challenged ad is *false on its face.*[129] If actually false, the statement warrants relief without an analysis of consumer reaction to the ad.[130]

The Lanham Act, however, encompasses more than just literal falsehoods. "A statement actionable under the Lanham Act may be an affirmatively misleading statement, a partially incorrect statement, or a statement which

---

126. *Id.* at 782 n.10.
127. *See* text accompanying *supra* notes 50–53.
128. McNeilab v. American Home Products Corp., 501 F. Supp. 517, 529 (S.D.N.Y. 1980).
129. R. J. Reynolds Tobacco Co. v. Loew's Theatres, Inc., 511 F. Supp. 867, 874 (S.D.N.Y. 1980).
130. American Brands, Inc. v. R. J. Reynolds Tobacco Cc., 413 F. Supp. 1352, 1356 (S.D.N.Y. 1976).

is untrue as a result of a failure to disclose a material fact."[131] The issue revolves around the ad's meaning as perceived by its viewers, not its literal truthfulness.[132]

b. *Public Perception of the Advertisement*

To recover in a section 43(a) action, the ad need not be literally false. The Court of Appeals for the Second Circuit stated that "were it otherwise, clever use of innuendo, indirect intimations, and ambiguous suggestions could shield the advertisement from scrutiny precisely when protection against such sophisticated deception is most needed."[133]

Furthermore, the public's reaction to the ad must be tested: "The public's reaction to the ad will be the starting point in any discussion of the likelihood of deception. . . . If an ad is designed to impress . . . customers . . . the reaction of that group will be determinative."[134] In addition, courts must consider the ad in its entirety and not engage in disputatious dissection. "The entire mosaic should be viewed rather than each tile separately."[135]

If not false on its face, plaintiff must prove the ad's tendency to mislead or deceive[136] by a preponderance of the evidence.[137] Plaintiffs meet this burden by introducing consumer survey data.[138] No established quantitative measure exists to determine the degree to which an ad must mislead or deceive for a plaintiff to prevail under the Lanham Act. A qualitative showing that a "not insubstantial" number of consumers receive a false or misleading impression from the ad is sufficient.[139]

Decisions to date find a claim wrongly perceived by one percent of consumers insubstantial, and a misleading representation perceived by fifteen percent of consumers not insubstantial.[140] Consumer survey information,

---

131. U-Haul International Inc. v. Jartran, Inc., 522 F. Supp. 1238, 1247 (D. Ariz. 1981). For an example of a statement untrue as a result of a failure to disclose a material fact, see Philip Morris, *supra* note 114. *See also* Lee, *supra* note 56, at 633.; AHP, *infra* note 133; American Brands, Inc. v. R. J. Reynolds Tobacco Co., 412 F. Supp. 1352, 1357 (S.D.N.Y. 1976).
132. American Brands, Inc. v. R. J. Reynolds Tobacco Co., 413 F. Supp. 1352, 1357 (S.D.N.Y. 1976).
133. American Home Products v. Johnson & Johnson, 577 F.2d 160, 165 (2d Cir. 1978) (hereinafter "AHP").
134. American Brands, Inc. v. R. J. Reynolds Tobacco Co., 413 F. Supp. 1352, 1357 (S.D.N.Y. 1976).
135. FTC v. Sterling Drug, Inc., 317 F.2d 669, 674 (2d Cir. 1963); R. J. Reynolds Tobacco Co. v. Loew's Theatres, Inc., 511 F. Supp. 867, 875 (S.D.N.Y. 1980).
136. American Home Products v. Abbott Labs, 522 F. Supp. 1035, 1038 (S.D.N.Y. 1981); U-Haul International, Inc. v. Jartran, Inc., 522 F. Supp. 1238, 1248 (D. Ariz. 1981).
137. *Id.*
138. *Id.*
139. McNeilab v. American Home Products, Corp., 501 F. Supp. 517, 528 (S.D.N.Y. 1980).
140. Marx, *supra* note 49, at 418.

therefore, plays an integral role in any action under section 43(a).[141]

Consumer Survey Data. Plaintiffs use, essentially, two types of consumer surveys in these cases:

(1) "forced exposure" tests in which the people being tested view the ad once or twice, usually in a theatre-type room, and then fill out questionnaires regarding their interpretation of the ad;[142] and

(2) "day after recall" tests, in which phone surveys are conducted the day after the running of an ad, and those people who viewed the ad are asked to interpret the ad.[143]

Courts favor the first test because the audience pays close attention to the programs and ads. Consequently, the viewer can accurately interpret the ad's message. An injunction will issue if plaintiff can show that a "not insubstantial" number of viewers misperceived the ad.[144]

Methodology of Consumer Tests. Plaintiff's success may also lie in successfully attacking the defendant's methodology when defendant conducts product comparison tests and advertises the results. The important question asks whether the test itself may be false or misleading due to its methodology.[145] When ads make subjective preference claims, courts carefully analyze the test's design. Consumer preference tests generally take two forms:

(1) blind monadic testing, where the subject tests one product and rates it on a qualitative scale;[146] and

(2) comparison testing, where the subject tries more than one product over an extended period of time and develops a preference for one.

The propriety of blind monadic testing for comparative ads prompts criticism[147] because no real comparison is made. Plaintiff can show the faultiness of methodology by introducing a better, more accurate test and its results.[148] Even when confronted with comparison testing, the court must analyze the defendant's report of the test results.

In *Philip Morris, Inc. v. Loew's Theatres, Inc.* Loew's had smokers try one of its cigarettes (Triumph) and then one of plaintiff's cigarettes (Merit). The smoker rated the two in comparison to each other. The test results showed

---

141. American Brands, Inc. v. R. J. Reynolds Tobacco Co., 413 F. Supp. 1352, 1357 (S.D.N.Y. 1976); McNeilab v. American Home Products Corp., 501 F. Supp. 517, 525 (S.D.N.Y. 1980); Quaker State Oil Refining Corp. v. Burmah-Castrol, Inc., 504 F. Supp. 178, 182 (S.D.N.Y. 1980).
142. AHP, 577 F.2d 160 (2d Cir. 1978).
143. McNeilab v. American Home Products Corp., 501 F. Supp. 517, 529 (S.D.N.Y. 1980). AHP, 577 F.2d 160, 168 (2d Cir. 1978).
144. McNeilab v. American Home Products Corp., 501 F. Supp. 517, 528 (S.D.N.Y. 1980); R. J. Reynolds Tobacco Co. v. Loew's Theatres, Inc., 511 F. Supp. 867, 876 (S.D.N.Y. 1980).
145. R. J. Reynolds, 511 F. Supp. 867, 875 (S.D.N.Y. 1980).
146. Vidal Sassoon, Inc. v. Bristol-Myers Co., 661 F.2d 272 (2d Cir. 1981).
147. *Id.* at 271.
148. American Home Products v. Abbott Labs, 522 F. Supp. 1035, 1045 (S.D.N.Y. 1981).

that 36 percent of those surveyed preferred Triumph (Loew's), 24 percent said they tasted the same, and 40 percent preferred Merit.[149] Loew's ad proclaimed that "Triumph beats Merit" because sixty percent of those surveyed said that Triumph tastes as good as or better than Merit.[150] Loew's, however, withheld the fact that 64 percent said that Merit tasted as good as or better than Triumph.[151]

The court, unimpressed with Loew's claim that the ads could not be enjoined because of literal truthfulness, indicated that deceptiveness is the primary issue.[152] The court stated:

> "The misleading implication resulting from the use of the percentages favoring Triumph and the omission of the similar percentage for Merit is demonstrated by the results [of a consumer reaction survey conducted by plaintiff]. . . . Though the statement is statistically accurate, the omission of the percentages established by the [taste] Test with their clear implication with respect to taste has caused the ads to be deceptive to the general public. . . ."[153]

The court, in granting the injunction, stated that the ad's deceptiveness injured both the public and plaintiff regardless of its literal truth.

Generally, plaintiff shoulders the burden of showing that the test's methodology is suspect in some way.[154] Plaintiff must develop specific criticisms of the test's methodology,[155] which can be accomplished by conducting a better, more reliable test. Defendant then must show that the methodology is sufficient to withstand a challenge that the ad is misleading.[156]

D. "My Product is Better" or "Their Product Stinks"; How Far Can a Competitor Go?

Courts applying section 43(a) in actions not dealing with palming off or false designation of origin must determine what constitutes actionable statements. Statements merely claiming the superiority of one's product are

---

149. Philip Morris, Inc. v. Loew's Theatres, Inc., 511 F. Supp. 855, 858 (S.D.N.Y. 1980).
150. *Id.*
151. *Id.*
152. *Id.* at 858.
153. *Id.*
154. American Home Products v. Abbott Labs, 522 F. Supp. 1035, 1039 (S.D.N.Y. 1981).
155. *Id.*
156. American Home Products v. Abbott Labs, 522 F. Supp. 1035, 1039 (S.D.N.Y. 1981).

usually considered "puffing."[157] Whether the ad employs "puffing" or actionable falsity raises a factual issue.[158] Statistical, head-to-head comparisons cannot be characterized as "puffing." Such statements represent more than defendant's opinion.[159]

Courts rely on consumer surveys when determining whether the ad's language amounts to mere puffing or an actionable falsehood.[160] In *American Home Products v. Abbott Labs,* Abbott advertised a hemorrhoid remedy that "stops pain immediately." The court found that most consumers perceived "stops" as meaning "ceases or ends," when Abbott actually meant the product *reduced or relieved* pain.[161] The court enjoined the ad due to its misleading nature.[162]

The persuasiveness of T.V., radio, and print ads contributed to the change in attitude toward puffing.[163] The impressive nature of these ads provides an air of reliability not associated with the "salesman's pitch," which puffing was developed to cover.[164] The modern setting, where slick ads have an aura of veracity,[165] antiquates the old justification for allowing puffing, explained as a realization "that men will naturally overstate the value and qualities of the articles which they have to sell. All men know this, and a buyer has no right to rely upon such statements."[166] Although still available as a defense, courts no longer allow advertisers to make unfounded, opinion-like puffing statements about their products. Courts focus more on the ad's literal falsity and/or misleading nature.[167]

The strictness trend is less prevalent when the defendant merely fails to disclose information.[168] A court permitted a defendant to withhold information in *Alfred Dunhill Ltd. v. Interstate Cigar Co.*[169] Dunhill, a manufacturer of tobacco, shipped tobacco across the Atlantic Ocean. Water leakage damaged the shipment of tobacco. Dunhill received insurance compensation, and the insurance company sold the damaged goods to a salvage company. Interstate, aware of the damage, bought the tobacco and sold it at retail over Dunhill's

---

157. In order to be classified as "puffing" the representation must be "offered and understood as an expression of the seller's opinion only. . .on which no reasonable man would rely." PROSSER, HANDBOOK OF THE LAW OF TORTS 722 (4th ed. 1971).
158. Marx, *supra* note 49, at 403.
159. U-Haul International, Inc., v. Jartran, Inc., 533 F. Supp. 1238 (D. Ariz. 1981).
160. Marx, *supra* note 49, at 403.
161. *Id.*
162. *Id.*
163. *Id.*
164. *Id.*
165. *Id.* at 404.
166. Kimball v. Bangs, 144 Mass. 321 (1887).
167. Marx, *supra* note 49, at 404.
168. *Id.* at 406.
169. Alfred Dunhill Ltd. v. Interstate Cigar Co., 499 F.2d 232 (2d Cir. 1974).

requests that the tobacco be labelled as salvaged.[170]

The District Court held that Interstate's omission constituted false representation and, therefore, violated the Act.[171] The Court of Appeals reversed, however, stating that a mere failure to disclose did not give rise to an actionable wrong under section 43(a).[172] Although still good law, *Dunhill* is restricted by recent cases holding that section 43(a) applies to ads with the tendency to deceive.[173]

Finally, no action lies under section 43(a) for statements made about plaintiff's product, no matter how disparaging the statement, unless defendant also makes claims about his/her own product in the ad.[174] Although some commentators argue that statements about plaintiff's product should be actionable,[175] the rule remains that false statements about plaintiff's product only do not support an action under section 43(a). The rule instructs that "as long as the advertiser's claim is true, his comparison may be disparaging, it may be derogatory, it may be downright nasty."[176] Aggrieved parties, however, maintain a remedy under these circumstances, because they can rely on common law disparagement actions or petition the networks to refrain from airing such ads.[177]

IV. CONCLUSION

The law of unfair competition has evolved substantially since 1900 and the landmark *American Washboard* case of that year. Everything from consumer preferences to pressure from foreign companies influenced the law's changes.

The doctrines evolved slowly. The evolution continues, moving toward an acceptable standard of recovery for aggrieved competitors. Through various channels, including protests to the networks, appeals to the National Advertising Division of the Council of Better Business Bureaus, and private litigation, a competitor believing that a comparative ad harmed his/her product or his/her company's good will can obtain the most important relief available in this area—an injunction to abate the ad.

170. *Id.* at 233–34.
171. Alfred Dunhill Ltd. v. Interstate Cigar Co., 364 F. Supp. 366, 372 (S.D.N.Y. 1973).
172. Dunhill, 499 F.2d 232, 236 (2d Cir. 1974).
173. Marx, *supra* note 49, at 407.
174. *See* text accompanying *supra* note 120. *See also,* Dietene, 415 F.2d 1279 (7th Cir. 1969); Ragold, 506 F. Supp. 117 (N.D. Ill. 1980).
175. *See* text accompanying *supra* notes 121–126.
176. Nye, *In Defense of Truthful Comparative Advertising,* 67 TRADE-MARK REP. 353 (1977).
177. The networks established guidelines for comparative ads stating that such ads should not disparage or unfairly attack competitors or their products. *See supra* note 18. However, in light of the fact that networks air ads permitting competitors to make statements such as those seen in the text accompanying *supra* note 23, it would appear the networks loosely enforce their guidelines.

To recover under section 43(a), plaintiff must show that: (1) defendant is a person (2) who used false descriptions and misrepresentations (3) in connection with goods and services, (4) which defendant caused to enter commerce. (5) Plaintiff must be a person (6) who believes himself/herself to have been in fact damaged by defendant's misdescriptions or misrepresentations.[178] In addition, to obtain injunctive relief, plaintiff must show: (1) a likelihood of success on the merits, (2) that (s)he has suffered, and is likely to continue to suffer, irreparable injury to his/her market share or the good will of his/her product, and (3) that the balance of equities tips decidedly in favor of granting equitable relief.[179]

Although courts generally withhold standing from consumers, the FTC's recent trend away from consumer protection calls for a re-evaluation of that stance. The consumer is, ultimately, the party most injured by false advertisements (whether comparative in nature or not). Courts should show less concern with equitable doctrines among the parties to the suit and more awareness of the public policies involved.

The continued expansion of comparative advertising shows no signs of slowing. Courts, in order to facilitate intelligent purchase decisions, must dedicate their resources to insure truth and accuracy in advertising.

---

178. Colligan v. Activities Club of New York, Ltd., 442 F.2d 686 (2d Cir. 1971).
179. Thomson, *supra* note 15, at 391.

GARY B. WILCOX
DOROTHY SHEA
ROXANNE HOVLAND

Alcoholic Beverage Advertising and the Electronic Media

Gary B. Wilcox is Assistant Professor of
Advertising at The University of Texas at
Austin. He holds a B.B.A. in marketing
and an M.A. in communications from The
University of Texas at Austin. He earned a
Ph.D. in mass media from Michigan State
University. His research has appeared in
such publications as the *Journal of Advertising* and the *Journal of Advertising
Research.*
Dorothy J. Shea received her M.A. in
advertising from The University of Texas
at Austin, in 1985. She has a B.A. in
American history from Temple University
in Philadelphia. Currently, Ms. Shea
works with the Marsh & Box Company in
Austin, Texas.
Roxanne Hovland is Assistant Professor
of Advertising at The University of Texas
at Austin. She holds a B.A. in advertising
from The Univesity of Florida. Ms.
Hovland earned an M.S. in advertising
and a Ph.D. in communication from The
University of Illinois. Her research
publications have appeared in the *Proceedings* of the American Academy of
Advertising and the *Journal of
Macromarketing.*

In April of 1985, the Federal Trade Commission (FTC) rejected a petition
seeking restrictions on advertising of aclcoholic beverages.[1] Submitted by

---

1. *FTC Brings Cheer to Alcohol Marketers*, ADVERTISING AGE, April 22, 1985, at 14.

several citizens' groups including SMART (Stop Marketing Alcohol on Radio and Television), its parent organization, the Center for Science in the Public Interest, the National Council on Alcoholism, and the National Congress of Parents and Teachers, the petition recommended curbing alcohol advertisements and eliminating broadcast advertising for beer and wine entirely.

These groups claimed that such advertising is misleading and promotes increased consumption of addictive substances. Due to the content and the number of alcohol advertising messages, proponents of the ban see advertising as a contributor to aclcohol abuse and the attendant tragic consequences. They cite as evidence the parallel increases in alcohol advertising expenditures and consumption of beer, wine and spirits.[2] In contrast, broadcasters and advertises argue that a ban would violate first amendment rights. They further refute that increased advertising expenditures have led to increased per capita consumption.[3]

In rejecting the petition, the FTC concurred with the latter argument, pointing to a lack of evidence for the contention that advertising stimulates consumption. Moreover, according to the FTC, even if advertising was found to significantly affect consumption, it would be insufficient grounds to warrant regulation on the basis of deception or unfairness as alcohol abuse does not necessarily result from increased consumption.[4] The FTC also questioned whether further activity concerning alcohol advertising might unnecessarily overlap that of the Bureau of Alcohol, Tobacco, and Firearms of the Department of Justice.[5]

Following a brief look at alcoholic beverage advertising in its current form and related marketing principles, recent empirical studies concerning the relationship between alcohol beverage advertising levels and the consumption of such beverages will be presented. The major portion of this article concerns the *Oklahoma Telecasters*[6] and *Capital Cities Cable, Inc.*[7] cases and earlier cases of a similar nature, focusing on the federal and state issues involved. Viewed in this context, justification for the FTC's decision becomes clear indeed.

I. ADVERTISING/MARKETING OF BEER AND WINE

Today, with the wide variety of beers targeted at all segments of the population, advertising is considered essential to the success of individual brands.

---

2. *State Legislators Push for Alcoholic Ad Ban*, RADIO NEWS, July 20, 1984, at 1, 2.
3. Gay, *TV Fights Beer Ban Talk*, ADVERTISING AGE, November 8, 1984, at 1, 38.
4. *Supra* note 1.
5. *Id.*
6. Oklahoma Telecasters Association v. Richard A. Crisp, 8 MEDIA L. REP. 1097 (1982).
7. Capital Cities Cable, Inc. v. Crisp, 10 MEDIA L. REP. 1873 (1984).

According to industry experts, beer advertising is predominantly an exercise in building images, and television is considered an excellent medium for this purpose. In 1984, for example, beer and wine expenditures for radio and TV were about $920 million in the U.S. and much of that came from the six major brewers making spot and national televison buys.[8]

The marketing of wine is slightly different. Traditionally, wine advertisers have relied on print and radio to select specific target audiences. Thus, the question of broadcast regulation of wine advertising has not been an issue. More recently, however, industry experts have reported print to be too selective, and some are opting for cable television buys. Notes one observer, "We don't buy cable for the sake of buying cable. We feel it is a good medium to reach people who drink wine." This trend toward cable use indicates that wine advertising is likely to come under the scrutiny of ban proponents in the future.[9]

II. ALCOHOL ADVERTISING AND CONSUMPTION

To date, there are only a few reports of empirical studies examining the effects of alcohol advertising and no clear scientific evidence that alcohol advertising increases alcohol beverage consumption, much less abuse.

Bourgeois and Barnes assembled data on levels of per capita consumption of beer, wine, and spirits for persons ages fifteen years and older, for each of the ten provinces of Canada for each year from 1951 to 1974.[10] Obtaining the four dependent variables of per-capita consumption of absolute alcohol from beer, wine, distilled spirits, and total per-capita consumption of absolute alcohol, the researchers divided the independent variables, the possible causes of consumption, into three groups: the controllable marketing variables, the semi-controllable nonmarketing variables, and the noncontrollable variables.

The research concentrated on the following controllable marketing variables: print advertising, broadcast advertising, price index, relative price index, tax index, number of liquor stores, provincial minimum drinking age and introduction of the breathalyzer. The major conclusion of the experiment was that many factors "influence alcohol consumption levels, but more variance in per-capita consumption is explained by the uncontrollable variables than is explained by the controllable marketing variables."[11] This suggests that alcohol consumption "is influenced more by uncontrollable variables than

8. Colford, *White House Offers Rx for Alcohol Ads*, ADVERTISING AGE, March 25, 1985, at 10.
9. Reed, *Wine Marketing: The Media*, ADVERTISING AGE, January 16, 1984, at M35.
10. Bourgeois and Barnes, *Does Advertising Increase Alcohol Consumption?* 19, No. 4 JOURNAL OF ADVERTISING RESEARCH 19 (1979).
11. *Id.* at 19, 28.

by those variables over which marketers and policy makers might exercise control in the short run."[12]

Bourgeois and Barnes found "significant relationships between the levels of print and broadcast advertising and per-capita consumption of beer, wine, and spirits, but the directionality of these relationships were different across models." The effect of this difference in directionality is that "no significant relationship is observed between the advertising variables and the level of per-capita consumption of total absolute alcohol."[13] The authors state that the study "produced little evidence to support the claim that the level of per-capita consumption of alcoholic beverages in Canada is influenced by the volume of advertising for those products."[14]

Ogborne and Smart studied the effects of restriction of alcohol advertisements in Manitoba, Canada and the United States, using statistical data on alcohol consumption.[15] The Manitoba government introduced new regulations on advertising in 1974, which removed beer advertisements from the Province's electronic and print media. The results demonstrated that "there is little that per-capita beer consumption has changed in any way since beer advertising ceased to feature in the Manitoba media. A time-series analysis confirmed what is clear from visual inspection, namely, that beer consumption has not decreased since beer advertisements were withdrawn from the media."[16]

In the study done in the U.S., Ogborne and Smart classified fifty states according to the restrictiveness of their controls on newspaper and magazine advertising of alcoholic beverages. The results showed that "advertising restrictions were unrelated to per-capita beer, wine or spirit consumption, to total consumption or to alcoholism rate."[17] The authors suggest that such restrictions "should be given a low priority among possible solutions to problems of restraining per-capita alcohol consumption."[18]

Blane and Hewitt noted that "examination of what is known about advertising in relation to sales and marketing leads to no clear-cut conclusions concerning its effect on consumption."[19] Although the authors acknowledge that it is "nevertheless evident that for every added dollar spent on liquor advertising during the past twenty years, there has been a directly proportional

12. *Id.* at 28.
13. *Id.*
14. *Id.*
15. Ogborne and Smart, *Will Restrictions on Alcohol Advertising Reduce Alcohol Consumption?* 75, No. 3 BRITISH JOURNAL OF ADDICTION 293 (1980).
16. *Id.* at 294/95.
17. *Id.* at 295.
18. *Id.*
19. Blane and Hewitt, *Alcohol, Public Education and the Mass Media: An Overview* 5, No. 1 ALCOHOL, HEALTH AND RESEARCH WORLD 11 (1980).

increase in liquor sales and consumption," it is quite unclear "whether one causes the other or both are largely determined by other trends in society."[20] They cite the fact that "sophisticated regression analyses of cigarettes and liquor indicate that tremendous changes in advertising are necessary to make much difference in overall consumption."[21] Although it appears that advertising is not a primary factor in raising consumption of package goods like alcoholic beverages, "it may nevertheless have considerable influence in maintaining levels."[22] The authors conclude that more research is needed before "one can say with certainty that alcohol programming increases alcohol consumption."[23]

Smart and Cutler examined the effects of a ban on alcoholic beverage advertising over a period of fourteen months in British Columbia.[24] Their results: "In general, the yearly per-capita consumption data do not show any striking effects of the ban on sales. . . .The beer consumption decrease was not only statistically insignificant, but it was also quite small in percentage terms, only three percent below consumption of all non-ban months studied."[25]

In their conclusion, Smart and Cutler assess the ban as follows:

> The data presented lent little support for the view that the British Columbia advertising ban reduced alcohol consumption. Both the yearly and monthly analyses of beer, wine and spirit consumption show no substantial effect of the ban. If there was a yearly effect on beer, wine or spirits, it must have been too small to detect. . . .The monthly data for beer and liquor sales show virtually no sign of a ban effect. . . .To date, there is still no evidence on the effects of a well-supported and well-policed ban on (the advertising) of alcoholic beverages.[26]

In summary, these empirical results have generally pointed to the lack of evidence positively linking bans of alcoholic beverage advertising with reduced alcohol consumption.

20. *Id.*
21. *Id.*
22. *Id.* at 12.
23. *Id.*
24. Smart and Cutler, *The Alcohol Advertising Ban in British Columbia: Problems and Effects on Beverage Consumption*, 71, No. 1 BRITISH JOURNAL OF ADDICTION 13 (1976).
25. *Id.* at 20.
26. *Id.* at 20–21.

III. RECENT LEGAL DEVELOPMENTS

A. Central Hudson

In *Central Hudson and Gas Corp. v. Public Service Commission*,[27] the Supreme Court adopted a four-part balancing test to determine the validity of any regulation of commercial speech.

From *Central Hudson*, commercial speech must meet the following criteria to receive first amendment protection:

(1) It must at least concern lawful activity and not be misleading;

(2) It must be determined whether the asserted governmental interest to be served by the restriction on commercial speech is substantial;

(3) If both inquiries yield positive answers, it must then be decided whether the regulation directly advances the governmental interest interest.[28]

Though it significantly altered the law of commercial speech, the cases provided few standards for applying its four-part test. It did not allocate the burden of proof on each of the four parts, and it failed "to define what constituted sufficient proof to prevail on the four determinatins."[29] The Court's holding and its use of the precedent do provide some needed guidelines, yet many issues continue to remain open for determination.

Nevertheless, questions are raised about a ban when evaluated along the third and fourth criteria of the *Central Hudson* test. In order for a ban to be deemed both in the interests of reducing alcohol cunsurnption (the third criterion) and not unnecessarily extensive in serving that interest (the fourth criterion), proof of its effectiveness in reducing consumption is required. Given the empirical findings obtained thus far, a ban would be inappropriate based on the *Central Hudson* test.

B. Oklahoma Telecasters

While Oklahoma law permits consumption of alcoholic beverages, it allows only the advertising of beer within the state; wine and distilled spirit advertising is prohibited. Several cable television system operators in Oklahoma filed suit in the United States District Court for the Western District of Oklahoma for declaratory and injunctive relief against enforcement of Oklahoma's prohibition against cable operators' carrying out-of-state alcoholic

---

27. Central Hudson and Gas Corp. v. Public Service Commission, 447 U.S. 557 (1980).
28. Haefner and Haefner, *Freedom of Commercial Speech: The Special Case of Liquor Advertising*, PROCEEDINGS OF THE AMERICAN ACADEMY OF ADVERTISING 108 (1984).
29. Sackett, *Alcoholic Beverage Advertising and the First Amendment* 52 U. CIN. L. REV. 871, 873 (Summer 1983).

beverage commercials over their systems. The District Court granted summary judgment and a permanent injunction for the cable operators, ruling that the cable operators were probhibited by federal law from altering or modifying out-of-state signals and had no feasible method of deleting wine advertisements. Further, the ban was ruled an unconstitutional restriction on the cable operators' right to engage in protected commercial speech.[30]

When the district court first applied the *Central Hudson* test to this case, The first two parts were easily proven. In this first *Telecasters* case, *Oklahoma Telecasters Association v. Richard A. Crisp* (Crisp was Director of the Oklahoma Alcoholic Beverage Control Board), the district court remained unconvinced, however, that the ban on advertising directly advanced the interests of the state: "There is no evidence before the court that Oklahoma's ban on advertising is a direct means of preventing alcohol abuse or protecting the health, safety, or welfare of Oklahomans."[31] Examination of evidence showing that alcohol consumption had increased in spite of the ban, in conjunction with the fact that beer TV and radio commercials, and beer, wine, and spirits magazine advertisements that originate outside of Oklahoma were allowed, indicated to the court that the ban would not be a direct means to the state's end. Further, the court found the ban to be more extensive than necessary, and suggested other means of encouraging temperance, such as alcohol education.

When the *Oklahoma Telecasters* case was appealed, *(Oklahoma Telecasters Association, Cable Com-General Inc. v. Richard A. Crisp)*,[32] the U.S. Court of Appeals reversed the district court's ruling. The crucial question in this case was whether Oklahoma's prohibition against advertising of alcoholic beverages, as applied to the Appelles, violated their first amendment rights as guaranteed by the fourteenth amendment.

The resolution of the issue involved an examination of the relative interests at stake; that is, the court had to balance the right of the cable operators to engage in commercial speech against the right of Oklahoma to regulate commercial speech relating to alcoholic beverages throught he twenty-first amendment.[33]

The U.S. Court of Appeals had no problem with the first two parts of the *Central Hudson* test, but found that the ban did directly advance the state's substantial interest, a departure from the findings of the district court. The court held firmly to the belief that the entire purpose of advertising is to make sales and, indeed, liquor manufacturers would not spend money to advertise

---

30. Oklahoma Telecasters Association v. Richard A. Crisp, 8 MEDAL L. REP. 1097 (1982).
31. *Id.*
32. Oklahoma Telecasters Association CableCom-General, Inc. v. Richard A. Crisp, 9 MEDAL L. REP. 1089 (1983).
33. Haefner and Haefner, *supra* note 28.

if this were not a true assumption. In finding that the ban directly advanced the interests of the state in reducing the sale, consumption and abuse of alcoholic beverages, the court stated:

> As a matter of law, the prohibition against the advertising of alcoholic beverages is reasonably related to reducing the sale and consumption of those beverages and their attendant problems. The entire economy of the industries that bring these challenges is based on the belief that advertising increases sales. We therefore do not believe that it is constitutionally unreasonable for the State of Oklahoma to believe that advertising will not only increase sales of particular brands of alcoholic beverages but also of alcoholic beverages generally.[34]

The Court of Appeals also found the ban to be no more extensive than necessary because, even though this one type of advertising was banned for the broadcasters, they were still free to carry other types of advertising. In addition, the ban on alcoholic beverage advertising, though extensive, was not complete. On-site advertising was allowed, beer commercials could be rebroadcast, and print advertisements originating outside the state were not forbidden.[35]

The Court of Appeals decision in the *Oklahoma Telecasters* case was largely based upon the belief that there is a cause and effect relationship between advertising and the sale of liquor. However, that belief seems untenable when the empirical evidence is considered. The lack of scientific evidence for a causal relationship between alcohol advertising and sales leads to a conclusion that the bans on liquor advertising are an unjustified abridgement of the protection of commerical speech under the first amendment.

Additionally, there are two other points to consider. First, in light of the federal regulations and laws applicable to cable operators, Oklahoma's advertising prohibitions may be pre-empted with respect to cable operators. When Oklahoma's statute directly conflicts with federal law, it must give way. Secondly, commerce clause principles indicate that Oklahoma's law is of questionable validity. Oklahoma's prohibitions do not relate to the process of bringing alcohol advertising into the state, but rather seek to regulate speech about alcohol legally brought into Oklahoma. Oklahoma's ban is, therefore, not entitled to the special deference granted laws within the clear contemplation of the twenty-first amendment. Instead, the prohibition should be subjected to ordinary commerce clause analysis. Under such an analysis, Oklahoma's advertising ban must fail as an unreasonable burden on interstate commerce.[36]

34. *Supra* note 32.
35. Haefner and Haefner, *supra* note 28, at 109; Oklahoma Telecasters Association CableCom-General, Inc. v. Richard A. Crisp, 9 Medal L. Rep. 1089 (1983).
36. Haefner and Haefner, *supra* note 28, at 109.

On certiorari, the United States Supreme Court reversed the Court of Appeals decision, holding that the Oklahoma ban on cable alcoholic beverage advertising is pre-empted by federal law, as noted in the original *Telecasters* case.[37] Justice J. Brennan's opinion in this case, *Capital Cities Cable, Inc. v. Richard A. Crisp*,[38] noted that:

> (The) state's ban conflicted with FCC regulations, completely pre-empting regulation of "pay-cable" programming requiring that out-of-state television signals be carried and carried without deletion or alteration; and the Twenty-first Amendment did not save the ban from pre-emption, since the ban squarely conflicted with the accomplishment and execution of the full purposes of federal law, and the state's power to regulate liquor importation and sale was not directly implicated.[39]

Brennan continued his opinion as follows:

> Petitioners contend that Oklahoma's requirement abridges their rights under the First and Fourteenth Amendments and is pre-empted by federal law. Because we conclude that this state regulation is pre-empted, we reverse the judgement of the Court of Appeals...and do not reach the First Amendment question. We conclude that the application of Oklahoma's alcoholic beverage advertising ban to out-of-state signals carried by cable operators in that state is pre-empted by federal law and that the Twenty-first Amendment does not save the regulation from pre-emption.[40]

A discussion of the issues in the opinion is necessary. First, the twenty-first amendment does not save the advertising ban from pre-emption. The constitution allows that the states enjoy broad power under section two of the amendment to regulate the importation and use of intoxicating liquor within their borders. However, when a state does not attempt directly to regulate the sale or use of liquor, a conflicting exercise of federal authority may prevail. In such a case, the central question is whether the interests implicated by a state regulation are so closely related to the powers reserved by the amendment that the regulation may prevail, even though its requriements directly conflict with express federal policies.[41]

---

37. Note, *The Substantive Fallacy of the Twenty-First Amendment: A Critique of* Oklahoma Telecasters Association v. Crisp (10th Annual Tenth Circuit Survey: June 1, 1982 to May 31, 1983), 61 DEN. L.J. 252–53 (Spring 1984).
38. Capital Cities Cable, Inc. v. Crisp (1984). 10 MEDAL L. REP. 1873 (1984).
39. *Id.*
40. *Id.*
41. *Id.*

Here, Oklahoma's interest in discouraging consumption of intoxicating liquor is limited, since the state's ban is directed only at wine commercials appearing on out-of-state signals carried by cable operators, while the state permits advertisements for all alcoholic beverages carried in newspapers and other publications printed outside Oklahoma, but sold in the state. Furthermore, the state's interest is not of the same stature as the FCC's interest in ensuring widespread availability of diverse cable services throughout the United States.[42]

Concerning the question of whether Oklahoma's ban conflicts with the federal regulation of cable television systems so that it is pre-empted, the following points should be considered. First, federal regulations have no less pre-emptive effect than federal statues, and the power delegated to the FCC under the Communications Act of 1934 plainly includes authority to regulate cable television systems in order to ensure achievement of the FCC's statutory responsibilites.[43]

The FCC has for the past twenty years unambiguously expressed its intent to pre-empt state or local regulation of any type of signal carried by cable television systems. By requiring cable television operators to delete commercial advertising contained in signals carried pursuant to federal authority, the state has clearly exceeded its limited jurisdiction and has interfered with a regulatory area that the FCC has explicitly pre-empted.[44]

Secondly, Oklahoma's ban also conflicts with several specific FCC regulations requiring that certain cable television operators, such as the petitioners in the case, carry signals from broadcast stations located nearby in other states. Such signals must be carried in full, including all commercial advertisements. Similarly, Oklahoma's ban conflicts with FCC rulings permitting and encouraging cable television systems to import more distant, out-of-state broadcast signals which, under FCC regulations, must also be carried in full. Moreover, it would be a prohibitively burdensome task for a cable operator to monitor each signal it receives and delete every wine commercial. Thus, enforcement of Oklahoma's ban might deprive the public of the wide variety of programming options that cable systems make possible. Such a result is entirely at odds with the FCC's regulatory goal of making available the benefits of cable communications on a national basis.[45]

Finally, the Copyright Revision Act of 1976 establishes a program of compulsory copyright licensing that permits a cable operator to retransmit distant broadcast signals upon payment of royalty fees to a central fund, but re-

42. *Id.*
43. *Id.*
44. *Id.*
45. *Id.*

quires that the operator refrain from deleting commercial advertising from the signals. Oklahoma's deletion requirements force cable operators to lose the protection of compulsory licensing, or to abandon their importation of broadcast signals covered by the act. Such a loss of viewing options would thwart the policy identified both by Congress and the FCC of facilitating and encouraging the importation of distant broadcast signals.[46]

IV. CONCLUSIONS

For future regulation of alcoholic beverage advertising in the electronic media, three important issues are raised by the court decisions. First, from the *Capital Cities Cable, Inc.* decision, the alteration of imported cable signals from surrounding markets is in violation of federal regulations as administered by the FCC and the Copyright Revision Act of 1976.

Secondly, the restriction of truthful alcoholic beverage advertising on commercial radio and television based on the assumption that the advertising increases consumption and sales is scientifically unfounded. Clearly, the proponents of such a ban are unable to produce empirical evidence to support their position.

Third, in the absence of such evidence, it is likely that the ban either did, or would have, run afoul of the criteria of the *Central Hudson* test which state, in essence, that any restriction of commerical speech must serve its intended purpose and not be more extensive than needed.[47]

Alcohol abuse in the U.S. arises as a result of myriad social, cultural and demographic factors, of which advertising is only a part. Obviously, to eliminate broadcast advertising of beer and wine based on the assumption that it induces increased consumption and abuse is erroneous and, therefore, both inappropriate and a more extensive policy than needed.

The FTC's decision thus seems proper given the legal history and empirical evidence that pertain to alcoholic beverage advertising. Moreover, any future prohibition of alcohol advertising is unjustified at either the state or the federal level. The actions of SMART and the other petitioners were not in vain, however. Thanks to their vigorous efforts and the debate they stimulated, much needed attention has been focused on the problems of alcohol abuse as well as on the responsibilities of advertisers and media.

46. *Id.*
47. Central Hudson and Gas Corp. v. Public Service Commission, 447 U.S. 557 (1980).

ROXANNE HOVLAND
GARY B. WILCOX

The Future of Alcoholic Beverage Advertising*

Roxanne Hovland is an assistant
professor and Gary B. Wilcox an
associate professor in the department of
advertising at The University of Texas-
Austin.

Recent developments at the Supreme Court raise serious doubts about the
status of advertising under the first amendment. First, in a case concerning
a Puerto Rican law banning casino advertising to Puerto Rican citizens
(*Posados de Puerto Rico v. Tourism Co.*), the Court for the first time upheld
a ban on truthful advertising for a legal product.[1] Second, the elevation of
William Rehnquist—author of the majority decision in the Puerto Rican case
and a well-known critic of commercial speech rights—as Chief Justice of
the Supreme Court, in combination with an increasingly polarized Court,
may further weaken the already tenuous status of advertisers' rights to free
speech.[2]

* Other articles by the authors on the subject of alcoholic beverage advertising include:

Hovland & Wilcox, *Alcoholic Beverage Advertising in the Electronic Media and the First
Amendment,* PROCEEDINGS OF THE AMERICAN ACADEMY OF ADVERTISING (1986).
Wilcox, Vacker & Franke, *Alcoholic Beverage Advertising & Consumption in the United
States: 1964–1984,* Department of Advertising Working Paper #86-1, The Univer-
sity of Texas, Austin, Texas (Spring 1986).
Wilcox, Shea & Hovland, Capital Cities Cable: *Implications for Alcoholic Beverage Adver-
tising in the Electronic Media,* COMMUNICATIONS AND THE LAW (February 1986).
Wilcox, *The Effect of Price Advertising on Alcoholic Beverage Sales,* JOURNAL OF ADVER-
TISING RESEARCH (Oct./Nov. 1985).
Wilcox, *Implications of First Amendment Doctrine on Prohibition of Truthful Price Adver-
tising Concerning Alcoholic Beverages,* COMMUNICATIONS AND THE LAW (Spring 1981).

1. Colford, *High Court's Ruling Sets Back Ad Rights,* ADVERTISING AGE, July 7, 1986,
1.
2. Colford, *Justice Rehnquist Slams Ad 1st Amendment Shield,* ADVERTISING AGE,
June 30, 1986, 12; Lauter, *A New Polarization for the High Court,* THE NATIONAL
LAW JOURNAL, August 11, 1986, S-3.

The history of advertising and the first amendment shows that the present situation is unsurprising. Certainly, not all advertising has been considered worthy of protection. The landmark court decision of 1976 (*Virginia State Board of Pharmacy v. Virginia Citizens Consumer Council*) specifically identified false advertising as contrary to public interest and therefore unprotected.[3] Of greater interest from a first amendment standpoint, however, is the still undetermined status of otherwise "legal" advertising—non-deceptive advertising for legal products and services. The confusion resulting from this has been most dramatically illustrated by the ongoing battle concerning broadcast advertising for alcoholic beverages. Although the Federal Trade Commission (FTC) declined to institute a ban of advertising in the broadcast media, debate continues in a number of arenas, many at the state level.[4]

This article examines a series of cases on advertising and the first amendment. The list of cases, although not exhaustive, includes those that have been instrumental in shaping current treatment of advertising. Several key issues that run throughout this history are identified and used to assess the future of alcoholic beverage advertising, particularly in the electronic media.

I. RELEVANT FIRST AMENDMENT CASES

Valentine v. Chrestensen (1942). In 1942, an individual attempted to distribute handbills promoting tours of a U.S. Navy submarine for a fee. Told he was in violation of the New York City Sanitary Code, a legal battle ensued. Ultimately, the Supreme Court decision in the *Valentine* case defined absolutely commercial speech as outside protection of the first amendment. Since the primary purpose of the handbill was commercial, it was undeserving of first amendment protection.[5]

New York Times v. Sullivan (1964). Twenty-two years later, the Supreme Court made a step toward protecting commercial speech when it considered the content of an ad in *The New York Times* worthy of protection. Although the Committee to Defend Martin Luther King and the Struggle for Freedom in the South had paid for space in the paper, the content was deemed of great public interest. The commercial form of the speech did not invalidate the value of its content.[6]

Capital Broadcasting Co. v. Mitchell (1972). The Supreme Court was asked to assess the legality of the Public Health Cigarette Smoking Act of 1966, which banned advertising of cigarettes in any electronic medium. In upholding the Act, the Court based its decision largely on the unique nature

---

3. Knapp, *Commercial Speech, the Federal Trade Commission and the First Amendment,* 9 MEMPHIS STATE UNIVERSITY L. REV. 20 (1978).
4. *FTC Brings Cheer to Alcohol Marketers,* ADVERTISING AGE, April 22, 1985, 14.
5. Knapp, *supra* note 3, at 2–3.
6. *Id.* at 6–8.

of the electronic media. Unlike others, the broadcast media are intrusive by nature and defined as public property.[7]

Bigelow v. Virginia (1975). The Supreme Court took great strides in protecting commercial speech when it deemed a newspaper advertisement for an abortion referral agency of public interest and thus worthy of protection. Advertising per se is not unprotected—state interest in regulation must be balanced against the public interest in information.[8]

Virginia State Board of Pharmacy v. Virginia Citizens Consumer Council (1976). The balancing principle advanced in *Bigelow* was affirmed in 1976 when the Supreme Court accepted the importance to consumers of price advertising for prescription drugs. The Court, in pointing out the value of commercial speech in consumer decision making, accorded advertising a degree of first amendment protection greater than ever before. However, certain exceptions were specified:

1. "Where the time, place and manner but not the contents of speech are regulated" such as the control of handbills that may cause litter problems and;
2. where first amendment rights must be balanced against other societal interests, such as the case of false advertising which defeats the public's interest in receiving information.[9]

Justice Rehnquist was the only dissenter.

Central Hudson Gas & Electric Corp. v. Public Service Commission (1980). Justice William Rehnquist was again the only dissenter in a case concerning a regulation that completely banned advertising by an electric utility. The decision produced what many considered the Court's clearest treatment of advertising under the first amendment. In disallowing the regulation, the Court proposed a four-part test for balancing interests of consumers and the state. In order for a regulation of commercial speech to withstand judicial scrutiny, the following must be met:

1. It must concern lawful activity and not be misleading.
2. The asserted governmental interest must be substantial.
3. The regulation should directly advance the governmental interest;
4. and do so in a way that is not more extensive than is necessary to serve that interest.[10]

---

7. Schofield, *First Amendment Implications of Banning Alcoholic Beverage Ads on Radio and TV*, JOURNALISM QUARTERLY 535–536 (Autumn 1985).
8. Knapp, *supra* note 3, at 12–14.
9. *Id.* at 19–27.
10. Mandel, *Liquor Advertising: Resolving the Clash Between the First and Twenty-first Amendments*, 59 NEW YORK UNIVERSITY L. REV. 161.

The problem, of course, is how to uniformly apply the standards advanced in *Central Hudson*. Much was left up to interpretation.

Queensgate Investment Co. v. Liquor Control Commission (1982). The Supreme Court dealt commercial speech—and liquor advertising in particular—another blow in 1982. The Court dismissed an appeal directed to an Ohio ban of price advertising by liquor permit-holders. By not viewing the regulation as a first amendment violation, the importance of the twenty-first amendment giving states regulatory authority over advertising of alcoholic beverages was affirmed. In other cases, however, the Court asserted the importance of the first amendment over the twenty-first. The relationship between the two amendments is unclear.[11]

Bolger v. Youngs Drug Products Corp. (1983). A year later the Supreme Court applied the Hudson test to a federal statute prohibiting unsolicited mailing of contraceptive advertisements. The statute was struck down because it failed to significantly support the asserted governmental interests. In so doing, the principles of both *Virginia Board* and *Central Hudson* seemed to be reaffirmed.[12]

Capital Cities Cable, Inc. v. Richard A. Crisp (1984). The twenty-first amendment was faced again in a series of cases concerning an Oklahoma constitutional law prohibiting advertisements of alcoholic beverages within the state. The Supreme Court struck down the law, *not* based on first amendment grounds, but because the law conflicted with federal controls over cable television. The interests of the twenty-first amendment were subordinated to these federal controls as exercised by the Federal Communications Commission (FCC). Because of this finding, the Court stated that it was *unnecessary* to consider the first amendment question.[13]

Dunagin v. City of Oxford (1984), *Lamar Outdoor Advertising, Inc. v. Mississippi State Tax Comm.* (1984). In June 1984, the Supreme Court declined to hear two cases concerning a Mississippi law prohibiting the origination of alcoholic beverage advertising in the state in *any medium*. The Court let stand a Fifth Circuit Court of Appeals decision that upheld the constitutionality of the law. The circuit court had applied the *Central Hudson* test and found the law to serve the governmental interests and did not find it too extensive in doing so. In denying certiorari, the Supreme Court clearly, though indirectly, validated liquor advertising laws by the *Central Hudson* standard.[14]

Michigan Beer & Wine Wholesalers Assoc., Torkal Corp., Linda Bandy and Charles Mitchner v. Attorney General and Michigan Liquor Control Commission (1985). The Attorney General of Michigan challenged the Michigan Liquor Control Commission's authority to prohibit truthful price advertising

11. *Id.* at 168–174.
12. *Id.* at 165.
13. Schofield, *supra* note 7, at 537–538.
14. *Id.* at 538.

for beer. At the center of the controversy were certain administrative rules promulgated by the Commission, all of which imposed restrictions on the advertising of beer and wine by licensees of the Commission. The principal rule in question, while expressly authorizing most forms of general brand advertising of beer and wine, prohibited retailers from advertising the price of these products. In February 1982, the attorney general issued an opinion stating that

> [P]rohibiting truthful price advertising of alcoholic beverages was unconstitutional in that the rule (1) violated the freedom of commercial speech guaranteed by the First and Fourteenth Amendments to the United States Constitution and by Article 1 of the Michigan Constitution of 1963 and (2) constituted an unreasonable exercise of the Commission's police power authority. (142 Mich. App. 294, 370 N.W.2d 328 (1985))

In June of 1983, an Ingham County circuit court judge ruled that the attorney general did not have the power to repeal the ban in February 1982 and that the administrative rules prohibiting price advertising should be reimposed.

In February of 1986, the Supreme Court of Michigan reversed the lower court's ruling and held the Commission's rules "impermissible restraints on the freedom of commercial speech in violation of the First and Fourteenth Amendments of the United States Constitution." In reaching this decision, the Court relied on the four-part *Central Hudson* test. The regulations failed to pass the third criterion—whether the regulations directly advanced the state's interest in discouraging the artificial stimulation of alcohol consumption.

The Court agreed with the attorney general in acknowledging at least some correlation between general brand advertising of alcoholic beverages and levels of consumption. However, in light of the amount of advertising for brands of alcoholic beverages within the state, the Court found it difficult to perceive how the addition of the element of price could have any measurable impact on alcohol consumption. The Court concluded that the plaintiffs had failed to demonstrate how the regulations in question would directly advance temperance.[15]

Posados de Puerto Rico v. Tourism Co. (1986). The uncertain status of commercial speech is dramatically illustrated by the Supreme Court's decision to uphold a law that bans casino advertising to Puerto Rican citizens but allows such advertising to tourists. The Court relied on the *Central Hudson* test in its finding. However, in the majority decision, Justice Rehnquist based

---

15. Michigan Beer & Wine Wholesalers Assoc., Torkal Corp., Linda Bandy and Charles Mitchner v. Attorney General and Michigan Liquor Control Commission, 142 Mich. App. 294, 370 N.W.2d 328 (1985).

his argument on the notion that if sale of a product can be prohibited, then advertising of that product may be banned or restricted *even* if the sale of the product is allowed.[16] In other words, truthful advertising for legal products may be banned. Moreover, the application of the *Central Hudson* test in this case seems to shift the burden of proof to the opponents of the restriction.[17]

II. DISCUSSION

The pattern of court decisions concerning advertising and the first amendment, besides being inconsistent, does not bode well for alcoholic beverage advertising, particularly in the electronic media. Several issues point to this conclusion.

First, the concept of balancing, introduced in *Bigelow*, elaborated upon in *Virginia State Board of Pharmacy*, and most fully explained in *Central Hudson*, is very much operative. However, the process of balancing society's interests is still highly subjective. Without unduly equating the two sets of cases, the differing outcomes of *Central Hudson* and *Dunagin/Lamar* point to this. In the former case, a ban on advertising for an electric utility was deemed excessive. In *Dunagin/Lamar*, a restriction of any advertising for alcoholic beverage advertising in the state of Mississippi was found to serve substantial government interests in a manner that was not more extensive than necessary.

The implication is that advertising for electricity is more worthy of first amendment protection than advertising for alcoholic beverages. Within the class of nondeceptive advertising for legal products, different standards seem to apply. Part of the problem lies in the ambiguity of the last two parts of the *Central Hudson* test. The exercise of determining whether a regulation will serve a particular government interest is indeed subjective. Only more subjective is the process of ascertaining whether the law is more extensive than is necessary. The nature of the test suggests highly unpredictable outcomes.

It appears that the Court has reverted back to what has been called the "sliding scale approach" to first amendment review of commercial speech. In essence, the content of alcoholic beverage advertising is relatively less worthy of first amendment protection. This approach is reminiscent of that used in *New York Times* (1964), wherein the content of the advertisement was the deciding factor in whether it was protected. On this basis, restrictions on content of this kind require less scrutiny.[18] This is most obvious

16. Taylor *High Court, 5–4, Sharply Limits Constitutional Protection for Ads,* NEW YORK TIMES, July 2, 1986, 1.
17. Colford, *supra* note 1, at 62.
18. Steffey, *Tension Between the First and Twenty-first Amendments in State Regulation of Alcohol Advertising,* 37 VANDERBILT LAW REVIEW 1439–1451 (1984).

in the Supreme Court's decision in the Puerto Rican case, wherein the mere fact that casino gambling can be prohibited was sufficient to restrict advertising for gambling, although casinos are legal in Puerto Rico.

However, the *Central Hudson* test was passed to provide a stricter review process. Referred to as an "intermediate level of protection," the test, by requiring the state to show that the restriction directly promotes the state's interest, obviates the need for empirical support.[19] In practice, however, the *Central Hudson* test has been applied inconsistently. In some cases, it was not considered at all (*Capital Cities Cable*), while in others it was applied without the support of empirical evidence (*Dunagin/Lamar*). On the other hand, the decision in the recent Michigan case was based, in part, on empirical evidence.

The introduction and application of the *Central Hudson* test have thus failed to reduce the ambiguity in reviewing restrictions of commercial speech. The recent Puerto Rican case underscores this, as the burden of proof appears to have been shifted to the advertiser.

A second matter to consider is the special status accorded electronic media. The nature of electronic media as a basis for special regulation was shown in *Capital Broadcasting* in 1972. Because of the intrusive and public nature of these media, the Court fully accepted regulation of nondeceptive advertising for legal products. This notion was indirectly reaffirmed in the *Virginia State Board* case by allowing for control over the manner of presentation and for balancing of public interests.

For the most part, cable is treated similarly to broadcast media based on the idea that, like these media, cable access is scarce and therefore subject to governmental authority to ensure its use in the public interest.[20] Paradoxically, the basis for disallowing the Oklahoma restriction of alcohol advertising in *Capital Cities* was this same federal auhtority over cable. In this case, the state's power (through the twenty-first amendment) to control sales of alcohol was superceded by the FCC's authority over cable. At first glance, it would appear that, even though the first amendment issue was never addressed by the Court, the decision extends some protection to alcoholic beverage advertising in the electronic media.

However, in that same year, the Cable Communications Act of 1984 was passed. The Act "authorized municipalities to regulate cable systems by way of franchises and establishing standards for giving franchises."[21] The FCC was assigned a "relatively minor role" in exercising control over cable as the local franchising process is to provide primary control over, among other things, permissible contents of cable systems.[22] And, although the fran-

---

19. *Id.*
20. NELSON & TEETER, LAW OF MASS COMMUNICATIONS 609 (1986).
21. *Id.*
22. Myerson, *The Cable Communication Policy Act of 1984: A Balancing Act on the Coaxial Wires,* 19 GEORGIA L. REV. 551–555 (1985).

chising authority may not require specific programs, it may require the operator to better address the needs of the community through specialized programming. Moreover, the Act grants the power to municipal authorities to ban programming that is contrary to community standards.[23]

The Cable Act was passed, ostensibly, to provide a national cable policy. The end result may instead be a national patchwork of state and local policies that is certain to have impact over advertising on cable.

The first amendment implications of the new cable laws continue to unfold. The Supreme Court recently ruled unanimously in *Los Angeles v. Preferred Communications* (1986) that cable operators do have some first amendment protection. The Court struck down a lower court's decision allowing the city of Los Angeles to refuse a second cable company to operate in the area. Most communities have single cable franchises. The Cable industry has argued that these exclusive franchises and the laws governing them are in violation of cable operators' rights to free speech.[24]

Critical to this argument is whether the first amendment rights of cable operators are like those of newspapers, which enjoy broad rights to free speech, or those of the more narrowly defined rights of broadcasters. However, the Supreme Court did not determine this, so the first amendment rights of cable operators and, in turn, the rights of advertisers using this medium, are still unclear.[25]

The situation is further complicated by the vague relationship between state control over sales of alcoholic beverages and federal protection of speech. "The Supreme Court has never expressly addressed the impact of the Twenty-first Amendment on protection accorded commercial speech."[26] The cases in which the relationship between these two amendments has been addressed are mixed. The *Queensgate* decision seems to imply that states have considerable authority over advertising of alcoholic beverages through the twenty-first amendment. However, the decision failed to offer an analysis of how the amendments are related. On balance, the question of whether states' rights to regulate the sale of alcoholic beverages extend to the advertising of those beverages is uncertain.

In many respects, questions regarding federal versus state control represent the heart of the alcohol advertising issue. At least a dozen states are currently considering further study of, regulation of, or banning of alcohol advertising. The court cases that this attention has spawned, however, are a mixture of varying degrees of control over advertising of alcoholic beverages.

23. *Justices Unanimously Uphold Challenge in a Suit Over Cable TV Franchise,* NEW YORK TIMES, June 3, 1986, 12.
24. Gullett, *The 1984 Cable FlipFlop: From* Capital Cities Cable, Inc., v. Crisp *to the Cable Communications Policy Act,* 34 THE AMERICAN UNIVERSITY L. REV. 588–590 (1985).
25. *Id.*
26. Steffey, *supra* note 18.

Consider, for example, the outcomes of two recent cases. The Supreme Court ruled in *Capital Cities* that the Oklahoma law prohibiting alcoholic beverage advertising is inappropriate because it infringes on the federal control of cable. In *Dunagin/Lamar,* the Supreme Court let stand a Mississippi law prohibiting the origination of alcohol advertising within the state. The key difference between the two laws is that the Oklahoma law affected signals coming into the state, while the Mississippi law concerned only advertising originated in Mississippi. The message the Supreme Court is sending may be that states have much more discretion in controlling advertising within state boundaries, but less in controlling interstate advertising.

If the Michigan case were eventually put before the Supreme Court, the Court might let the decision stand simply because it concerns only intrastate advertising. Given that the regulations in question and the state supreme court's ruling pertain only to activities within state boundaries, a higher court may be unlikely to contest the Michigan decision.

One challenge to this may be if a higher court applied the *Queensgate* ruling as a precedent. In *Queensgate,* Ohio regulations prohibiting price advertising by liquor permit holders were deemed appropriate by the Supreme Court based on state rights conferred by the twenty-first amendment. On the surface, the two cases appear similar. However, as the Michigan Supreme Court carefully explains, the Michigan and Ohio regulations differ in several important respects. By comparison, the Michigan regulations were considered far more restrictive than those in *Queensgate.* Since the Michigan Liquor Control Commission attempted to restrict far more than on-site price advertising, *Queensgate* was found to be an inappropriate precedent.

A more serious challenge is the precedent set by the Puerto Rican case. Although the restrictions in question in the Michigan case were more narrowly focused (on the advertisement of alcohol prices) than those concerning advertising of casinos in Puerto Rico, the two cases are very similar in one important respect—the restrictions on advertising in both cases relate to products and activities that are themselves regulated. Applying Chief Justice Rehnquist's argument for restricting advertising by casinos to Puerto Ricans to the ban of price advertising of beer, the Michigan laws would appear perfectly legitimate. The lack of correlation between price advertising of alcoholic beverages and levels of consumption would be totally irrelevant.

The precedential value of the Puerto Rican case is still unclear, but certain factors evident in this and other cases seem determinant of regulation of commercial speech. Their ability to withstand judicial scrutiny seems to rest on: (1) the nature of the product advertised; (2) the use and application of the *Central Hudson* test; (3) whether the restrictions infringe on federal law; and (4) how stringent they are in controlling in-state advertising.

The national pattern of laws is highly uncertain, not only due to the apparent digression to the sliding scale approach of review, but also due to the increased emphasis on state control. The tension between federal and state controls is an ironic by-product of the trend toward deregulation. While this trend may have served to weaken federal authority, it may also serve to shift control to the states, as has been the case in cable regulation. Taken to an extreme, this could disperse the regulation of advertising to a state-by-state basis, similar to the pattern suggested by the three most recent cases. The legality of alcoholic beverage advertising in all media would depend upon the state in which it's disseminated. At the very least, placing advertising on a spot market basis would be a nightmare.

The fate of alcoholic beverage advertising is thus highly uncertain, as it rests on myriad legal and political factors at both the local and national levels. The Supreme Court's decision in the Puerto Rican case only further weakens the uncertain status of alcoholic beverage advertising as well as that of all truthful advertising for legal products. Given the Court's "spectacularly unpredictable" behavior toward commercial speech over the past decade and its increasingly polarized voting pattern, advertisers have good cause for concern.[27]

27. Abrams *Good Year for the Press, But Not for Advertisers,* THE NATIONAL LAW JOURNAL, August 11, 1986, S-14.

DENISE M. TRAUTH
JOHN L. HUFFMAN

The Commercial Speech Doctrine: *Posadas* Revisionism

Denise M. Trauth is a professor of
radio/television/film and John L. Huffman
is a professor of journalism at Bowling
Green State University.

The United States Supreme Court is currently in the process of radically redefining for the second time in a little over a decade the status of commercial speech *vis-a-vis* the first amendment, and it is doing so without any apparent public notice or commercial outcry. During the initial definition in 1942 in *Valentine v. Chrestensen*,[1] the Supreme Court ruled that commercial speech fell outside the ambit of first amendment protection. During the redefinition that began in 1975, the high Court gradually brought commercial speech under the constitutional ambit. This process reached its culmination in 1980 when the Supreme Court articulated a stringent test to be used in determining a state's ability to regulate commercial advertising.

A new and possibly revolutionary rendition of the commercial speech doctrine was delivered in 1986 when the Supreme Court without fanfare greatly expanded the scope of a state's power to limit advertising of a certain category of products or services.

This article will trace the evolution of the commercial speech doctrine since 1942 and discuss the profound implications of the most recent Supreme Court interpretation of the commercial speech doctrine.

---

1. 316 U.S. 52 (1942).

DENISE M. TRAUTH and JOHN L. HUFFMAN

I. HISTORY OF THE DOCTRINE

Valentine v. Chrestensen considered for the first time whether advertising was deserving of first amendment protection. The Supreme Court's answer was an unqualified "no." The Supreme Court ruled that all commercial speech was without the normal first amendment protection accorded almost all other speech. According to the Court, although the government could not prohibit a city's streets from being used for exercising freedom of expression, the United States Constitution "imposes no such restraint on government as respects purely commercial advertising."[2] This philosophy was to hold sway in the United States for some thirty-three years. In 1975, the Burger Court issued the first in a series of decisions that would eventually effectively reverse the *Valentine v. Chrestensen* philosophy.

In *Bigelow v. Virginia*,[3] the right of a newspaper to carry certain kinds of advertising was at issue. Although abortion during the first trimester of pregnancy had been held lawful by the Supreme Court in 1973, the state of Virginia continued to enforce a statute that prohibited encouraging abortions through advertising. Bigelow, managing editor of a weekly newspaper in Charlottesville, carried an advertisement for a New York abortion service and was convicted of violating the Virginia law.

In reversing Bigelow's conviction, the Supreme Court deviated from the earlier philosophy that had placed commercial speech beyond the scope of the first amendment, and established the doctrine that speech is not stripped of its constitutional protection merely because it appears in the form of a paid political advertisement.

Bigelow was important not only because it established protection for commercial messages but also because it justified that protection on the basis of the public's need for the information contained therein. In doing this, the Court erased the theretofore important legal distinction between speech falling into the political or public interest (i.e., speech necessary for the maintenance of democracy) and therefore protected category, and speech falling into the commercial (i.e., speech not related to self-government) and therefore non-protected category. Thus, the Court was admitting that, at times, political and commercial speech may be one and the same.

The rationale for affording constitutional protection to commercial speech was expanded in a second major case, *Virginia State Board of Pharmacy v. Virginia Consumer Council*.[4] Pharmacists had long been part of an elite group

---

2. *Id.* at 53.
3. 421 U.S. 809 (1975).
4. 425 U.S. 748 (1976).

of professionals including medical doctors, lawyers, and certified public accountants who refused to allow their membership to advertise their services under pain of expulsion from the professional society. This prohibition on advertising by pharmacists was challenged by a group of prescription drug users who felt their constitutional rights were violated by the advertising ban.

In supporting the consumers' contention, the Supreme Court stressed the fact that there are two addressees of first amendment protection: the disseminator and the receiver of information.

The Court reaffirmed this when it answered the assertion of the dissent that no right to receive the information that another wants to disseminate exists—at least not when the person objecting could obtain the information in another way, in this case by calling several pharmacists and asking about prices. The Court said:

> We are aware of no general principle that freedom of speech may be abridged when the speaker's listeners could come by his message by some other means, such as seeking him out or asking him what it is. Nor have we recognized any such limitation on the independent right of the listener to receive the information sought to be communicated.[5]

Although the dissent in this case seems to be focused on the distribution of information, the motivation behind this focus is an attitude toward commercial speech. In the thirty-four years that had intervened between this ruling and that of *Valentine v. Chrestensen*, the Court had faced the question of constitutional protection for commercial messages several times and had even begun in recent years to afford some such protection to advertisements, as in *Bigelow*. But it had never explicitly brought commercial speech under the mantle of the first amendment, partly because it had been able to attach the constitutional shelter to some "editorial" element in the advertising copy. In *Bigelow*, this requirement was satisfied by the Court's belief that some Virginians would be interested in the abortion advertisement due to a curiosity regarding the laws of other states.

In the *Board of Pharmacy* case, because no argument was made favoring protection for the advertisement based on viewing some element in it as editorial matter, the Court felt compelled to face the issue squarely.

5. *Id.* at 757.

Quoting prior cases that dealt with the issue of constitutional protection for commercial speech, the Court noted,

> Our question is whether speech which does "no more than promote a commercial transaction,"... is so removed from any "exposition of ideas"... and from "truth, science, morality and arts in general, in its diffusion of liberal sentiments on the administration of Government,"... that it lacks all protection. Our answer is that it does not.[6]

Although this case is usually remembered because it brought commercial advertising under first amendment protection and because it broke the barrier that had kept members of certain professional societies from advertising, *Virginia State Board of Pharmacy v. Virginia Citizens Consumer Council* went a long way toward securing the rights of consumers interested in receiving commercial messages. The Court did this by establishing the fact that many American's interest in commercial information may be keener than their interest in political issues. And this interest may be based not only on personal preferences but also on economic realities:

> Those whom the suppression of prescription drug price information hits the hardest are the poor, the sick and particularly the aged. A disproportionate amount of their income tends to be spent on prescription drugs; yet they are the least able to learn, by shopping from pharmacist to pharmacist where their scarce dollars are best spent. When drug prices vary as they do, information as to who is charging what becomes more than a convenience. It could mean the alleviation of pain or the enjoyment of basic necessities.[7]

The Court went on to upgrade the status of commercial information by explaining that the "public interest element," ordinarily considered a precondition to affording constitutional protection to any form of speech, is inherent in advertising of the sort of issue:

> Advertising, however tasteless and excessive it sometimes may seem, is nonetheless dissemination of information as to who is producing and selling what produce, for what reason, and at what price. So long as we preserve a predominately free

6. *Id.* at 762.
7. *Id.* at 763.

enterprise economy, the allocation of our resources in large measure will be made through numerous private economic decisions. It is a matter of public interest that those decisions, in the aggregate, be intelligent and well informed. To this end, the free flow of commercial information is indispensable ... And if it is indispensable to the proper allocation of resources in a free enterprise system, it is also indispensable to the formation of intelligent opinions as to how that system ought to be regulated or altered. Therefore, even if the First Amendment were thought to be primarily an instrument to enlighten public decision making in a democracy, we could not say that the free flow of information does not serve that goal.[8]

In this eloquent defense of the value of advertising in a capitalistic democracy, the Court seems to be retiring the dichotomy it begot thirty-four years before in *Chrestensen* between speech in the public interest category—speech which is necessary for the maintenance of democracy—and speech in the commercial category—speech which is not related to self-government.

Lest there be any question that this was indeed the intent of the Court, it took the opportunity to apply the reasoning of *Virginia State Board of Pharmacy* to another set of facts when it adjudicated a case dealing with advertising by attorneys, *Bates v. State Bar of Arizona.*[9]

Bates grew out of a complaint filed by the Arizona State Bar Association against two attorneys who violated a state supreme court disciplinary rule by advertising their legal services in a newspaper. The Arizona State Supreme Court upheld the bar association conclusion.

In reversion the decision of the high Court of Arizona, the Supreme Court began with an affirmation of its judgment in *Virginia State Board of Pharmacy* that speech should not be denied constitutional protection "merely because it proposed a mundane commercial transaction."[10] But the Court was not content to simply reassert protection for commercial speech. It went on to justify this protection by elaborating on the theme of consumer needs argued so effectively in the Virginia case:

> The listener's interest is substantial: the consumer's concern for the free flow of commercial speech often may be far keener than his concern for urgent political dialogue. Moreover,

8. *Id.* at 765.
9. 433 U.S. 350 (1977).
10. *Id.* at 364.

> significant societal interests are served by such speech. Adver-
> tising, entirely commercial, may often carry information of im-
> port to significant issues of the day... And commercial speech
> serves to inform the public of the availability, nature and prices
> of products and services, and thus performs an indispensable
> role in the allocation of resources in a free enterprise system
> [citations omitted].[11]

This acknowledgment on the part of the Court that when advertising fulfills the informational needs of consumers it serves an "indispensable" role in the smooth functioning of our free enterprise system reflects the Court's consciousness of an important fact: beginning in the second half of the 1970s, the top priorities of many Americans were economic conditions and economic survival.

The increase in constitutional protection for commercial speech was formalized in a 1980 case in which the Supreme Court promulgated a test to be used to determine the ability of a state to regulate advertising.

II. CENTRAL HUDSON

Central Hudson v. Public Service Commission[12] grew out of a 1973 order by the New York State Public Service Commission to the electric utilities companies in the state to cease all advertising that "promot[es] the use of electricity." The ban was originally based on the Commission's finding that "New York State does not have sufficient fuel stocks or sources of supply to continue furnishing all customer demands for the 1973–1974 winter."[13]

However, when fuel shortages had ceased three years later, the Commission, after requesting comments from the public, extended the prohibition in a 1977 Policy Statement. In its comments, Central Hudson Gas and Electric Corporation opposed the advertising ban on first amendment grounds. The policy statement divided advertising into two categories: (1) promotional advertising, intended to stimulate the purchase of utility services, and (2) informational advertising, designed to encourage shifts in consumption from peak demand times to periods of low electricity demand. Only the first type of advertising, promotional advertising, was prohibited by the ban.

Central Hudson challenged the Policy Statement in the New York State Courts, arguing that the Commission had restrained commercial speech in

---

11. *Id.*
12. 6 Media L. Rep. 1497 (1980).
13. *Id.* at 1498.

violation of the first and fourteenth amendments. The Commission's Policy Statement was upheld by the trial court, the intermediate appellate court, and the New York Court of Appeals. The case was then heard by the Supreme Court, which reversed the New York courts and found that the Policy Statement was indeed a violation of the first and fourteenth amendments.

The Supreme Court began its opinion in this case with a strong statement reiterating the first amendment protection adhering to commercial speech. Pointing to the line of cases beginning with *Bigelow*, the high Court stated, "Commercial expression not only serves the economic interests of the speaker, but also assists consumers and furthers the societal interest in the fullest possible dissemination of information."[14]

However, having reiterated the protection for this class of speech, the Court went on to point out the "commonsense distinction" between speech proposing a commercial transaction traditionally subject to government regulation and other kinds of speech.[15] Thus, the Court concluded that the protection available for a particular commercial expression is not as automatic as it is for other kinds of speech, but rather depends upon the nature both of the expression and of the government interest served by the regulation.

As a framework in which nature of expression and government interest can by analyzed, the Court advanced a four-part test. The ultimate use of the test was to determine when commercial speech is constitutionally immune from government regulation and when it is not.

Under this first part of the test, the courts must determine if the expression at issue is protected by the first amendment: at a minimum, it must concern a lawful activity and must not be misleading. If the advertisement concerns illegal activity or is misleading, no constitutional protection adheres to it at all and the analysis stops there. If, however, the expression passes this hurdle, analysis goes on the second part, in which the question is asked, "Is the government interest substantial?" If the answer to both these questions is positive, the court must then determine under the third part of the test if the regulation directly advances the government interest asserted. Fourthly, the court must ask whether the regulation is more extensive than is necessary to serve that interest.[16]

Application of this four-part test to the Public Service Commission's arguments led to the following analysis. The Commission had taken the position that Central Hudson's advertising was not inaccurate or related to an unlawful activity. But, the Commission reasoned, because Central Hudson

14. *Id.* at 1499.
15. *Id.*
16. *Id.* at 1501.

held a monopoly over the sale of electricity, the Commission's order restricted no commercial speech of any worth. The New York Court of Appeals "stated that advertising in a "noncompetitive market" could not improve the decision making of consumers. ... The court saw no constitutional problems with barring commercial speech that it viewed as conveying little useful information."[17] The Supreme Court did not agree, saying that this reasoning did not establish, as the first part of the test requires, that Central Hudson advertising was not commercial speech protected by the first amendment.

Then the Court went on to point out: "Even in monopoly markets, the suppression of advertising reduces the information available for consumer decisions and thereby defeats the purpose of the First Amendment."[18] According to the Court, whether or not to use the monopoly service or to what extent to use it were questions that consumer could answer with the help of information in advertisements. Finally, the Court concluded its application of the first part of the four-part test by stating: "[W]e may assume that the willingness of a business to promote its products reflects a belief that consumers are interested in advertising."[19] For all these reasons, in the opinion of the Supreme Court, Central Hudson prevailed in the application of the first part of the test.

The second part of the test inquired into the asserted state interest. The Public Service Commission offered two state interests as justification for its regulations. The first was energy conservation. The Supreme Court agreed that the state interest here was indeed substantial. The second state interest involved the aggravation of rate inequities caused by the failure of utility companies to base rates on marginal costs. Again, the Supreme Court agreed that state interest in inequities in utility rate structures was substantial. Thus the Commission was in compliance with the second part of the test.

The focus of the third part of the test was on the relationship between the asserted state interest and the advertising ban. The Supreme Court found a direct link between state interest in conservation and the advertising ban. "There is an immediate connection between advertising and demand for electricity. Central Hudson would not contest the advertising ban unless it believed that promotion would increase it sales."[20]

By contrast, the Court found the link between the advertising ban and Central Hudson's rate structure "at most, tenuous. ... Such conditional and remote eventualities simply cannot justify silencing appellant's promotional

17. *Id.*
18. *Id.*
19. *Id.* at 1502.
20. *Id.*

advertising."[21] The Court found no link between rate equity and efficiency on the one hand and an advertising ban on the other. Thus conservation emerged as the only ground that survived part three of the analysis.

Turning to the fourth part of the test, the Court said, "We come finally to the critical inquiry in this case: whether the Commission's complete suppression of speech ordinarily protected by the First Amendment is no more extensive than necessary to further the state's interest in conservation."[22]

In this section of its opinion, the Court concluded that the energy conservation rationale did *not* justify a ban on advertising, since the order reached all promotional advertising, regardless of the impact a particular advertisement may have had on total energy use. "In addition, no showing has been made that a more limited restriction on the content of promotional advertising would not serve adequately the state's interest."[23] For example, the Court pointed out, Central Hudson could have used advertising to promote the heat pump, which supposedly saves energy. The Court concluded its analysis by stating: "In the absence of a showing that more limited speech regulation would be ineffective, we cannot approve complete suppression of Central Hudson's advertising."[24]

The chief contribution of Central Hudson to the commercial speech doctrine is the enunciation of the above test, which can be used by lower courts in cases involving state regulation of advertising. The test clearly disallows a flat ban on a category of advertising, but would allow a ban if the state interest is substantial, if the relationship between the regulation and the state interest is direct, and if the regulation is the narrowest possible alternative.

Central Hudson can be read as a formalizing of the protection that the Supreme Court had invested in commercial speech beginning in *Bigelow*. However, it also introduced the notion that a state can ban some forms of advertising, a notion that came to fruition in a 1986 case arising out of advertising of casino gambling in Puerto Rico.

III. THE POSADAS CASE

Almost forty years ago, the government of Puerto Rico attempted to boost tourism by allowing the licensing of gambling casinos in the commonwealth. To accomplish this, it passed the Games of Chance Act of 1948. However, the legislature wished these casinos to be frequented only by tourists and not by native Puerto Ricans. Toward this end, in 1948 the legislature empowered

21. *Id.*
22. *Id* at 1502–03.
23. *Id.* at 1503.
24. *Id.*

the Economic Development Administration of Puerto Rico to issue and enforce regulations implementing various provisions of the Act. In 1970, the Tourism Company of Puerto Rico, a public corporation, assumed the regulatory powers of the Economic Development Administration. Two years later, the legislature amended the Act to codify a provision that "[n]o gambling room shall be permitted to advertise or otherwise offer their facilities to the public of Puerto Rico."[25]

In 1978, the appellant, Posadas de Puerto Rico Associates, a partnership that had obtained a franchise to operate a gambling casino in Puerto Rico, was fined by the Tourism Company for violating the advertising restrictions of the Act. The appellant protested the fines and in February of 1979, the Tourism Company issued to all casino franchise holders a memorandum interpreting the advertising restrictions. This memorandum broadly reiterated the prohibition of casino advertising in any form "which may be accessible to the public in Puerto Rico."[26] Pursuant to this memorandum, the Tourism Company assessed additional fines against the appellant. At this time, Posadas de Puerto Rico Associates paid the fines under protest and did not seek judicial review of the Tourism Company's decision.

In July of 1981, the appellant was again fined for violating the advertising restrictions. Faced with the threatened nonrenewal of its gambling franchise, the appellant paid the fine and then filed for a declaratory judgment against the Tourism Company in the Superior Court of Puerto Rico, seeking a judgment that the Act and the implementing regulations violated appellant's commercial speech rights.

The Superior Court found the regulation unconstitutional and issued a narrowing construction of the statute. The court pointed out that since the intent of the Act was to prohibit gaming rooms from advertising themselves to the citizens of Puerto Rico, only publicity campaigns aimed at residents were properly prohibited: "Advertisements of the casinos...are prohibited in the local publicity media addressed to inviting the residents of Puerto Rico to visit the casinos."[27]

However, regarding tourist advertising, the court said: "We hereby allow...advertising by the casinos addressed to tourists, provided they do not invite the residents of Puerto Rico to visit the casino, even though said announcements may incidentally reach the hands of a resident."[28]

The court then entered judgment declaring the appellant's constitutional rights had been violated by the Tourism Company's past application of the

---

25. Codified at P.R. Laws Ann., Tit. 15, S77 (1972.)
26. Posadas de Puerto Rico Associates v. Tourism Company, 13 Media L. Rep. 1033 (1986).
27. Id. at 1036.
28. Id.

advertising restrictions, but that the restrictions were not facially unconstitutional and could be sustained, as "modified by the guidelines issued by this court on this date."[29] Posadas appealed this ruling.

The Supreme Court of Puerto Rico dismissed Posadas's appeal, ruling that it did not present a substantial constitutional question. Appeal was then brought to the U.S. Supreme Court, which granted *certiorari* and held that the advertising restrictions, as narrowed by the Superior Court, were constitutionally valid.

In reaching this conclusion, Justice Rehnquist, writing for the five-person majority[30] applied the *Central Hudson* four-part test. Under the first part of this analysis, the justice asserted that commercial speech is entitled to first amendment protection if it (a) promotes a lawful act and (b) is not fraudulent or misleading. He found that the speech at issue passed both parts of this first element of the test; thus he proceeded to the three remaining steps.

The second part of this test involves assessment of the strength of the government's interest. The justice began by explaining the government's motivation for passing the regulations:

> The Tourism Company' brief before this Court explains the legislature's belief that "[e]xcessive casino gambling among local residents...would produce serious harmful effects on the health, safety and welfare of the Puerto Rican citizens, such as the disruption of moral and cultural patterns, the increase in local crime, the fostering of prostitution, the development of corruption, and the infiltration of organized crime."[31]

Recognition of this motivation led Rehnquist to assert: "We have no difficulty in concluding that the Puerto Rican Legislature's interest in the health, safety and welfare of its citizens constitutes a 'substantial government interest.' "[32]

Parts three and four of the *Central Hudson* test involve the question of fit. Part three requires a showing that the restriction directly advances the government interest identified in part two. Rehnquist easily concluded that "the answer to this question is clearly 'yes.' "[33] He found "reasonable" the legislators' belief that if advertising of casino gambling were allowed to be directed to local Puerto Ricans, this would lead to increased gambling on their part. It was the opinion of the majority that the very act of Posadas's bringing

---

29. *Id.* at 1037.
30. Included in the majority were former Chief Justice Burg___ and Justices White, Powell, and O'Conner. Dissenting were Justices Brennan, Stev____ ;, Marshall, and Blackmun.
31. MEDIA L. REP. 1033, 1039 (1986).
32. *Id.*
33. *Id.*

suit testified to the powerful impact of advertising: [T]he fact that appellant has chosen to litigate this case all the way to this Court indicates that appellant shares the legislature's view."[34]

The Court found it "clear beyond peradventure"[35] that the Puerto Rican regulations passed the fourth part of the *Central Hudson* test: the restriction must be no more extensive than necessary to achieve the government interest.

> The narrowing constructions of the advertising restrictions announced by the Superior Court ensure that the restrictions will not affect advertising of casino gambling aimed at tourists, but will apply only to such advertising when aimed at the residents of Puerto Rico.[36]

Posadas had contended that the first amendment required the government of Puerto Rico to reduce demand for casino gambling among residents, not by suppressing commercial speech that might encourage such gambling, but by promulgating additional speech designed to discourage it. The Supreme Court rejected this contention, asserting that it is up to the legislature to choose the policy it considers most effective in reducing demand for casino gambling. Thus the Court easily, and without a prolonged analysis, concluded that the regulations at issue in this case "pass muster under each prong of the *Central Hudson* test. We therefore hold that the Supreme Court of Puerto Rico properly rejected appellant's First Amendment claims."[37]

Finally the Court rejected the appellant's position that the challenged advertising restrictions were defective under the Court's holdings in *Carey v. Population Services Int'l*.[38] and in *Bigelow v. Virginia*.[39] In *Carey*, the Court had struck down a ban on advertisements of contraceptives. In *Bigelow*, as noted above, it reversed a criminal conviction based on the advertisement of an abortion clinic.

The Supreme Court pointed out that Posadas's argument ignored a crucial distinction between the *Carey* and *Bigelow* decisions and the instant case. According to the Court: "In *Carey* and *Bigelow*, the underlying conduct that was the subject of the advertising restrictions was constitutionally protected and could not have been prohibited by the State. Here, on the other hand, the Puerto Rico Legislature surely could have prohibited casino gambling by

---

34. *Id.*
35. *Id.* at 1040.
36. *Id.*
37. *Id.* at 1040
38. 431 U.S. 678 (1977).
39. 421 U.S. 809 (1975).

residents of Puerto Rico altogether."[40] The Court reasoned that the greater power to ban casino gambling necessarily included the lesser power to ban advertising of casino gambling.

Appellant also argued that having chosen to legalize casino gambling, under the first amendment Puerto Rico could not limit advertising of the activity. The Court disagreed: "[A]ppellant has the argument backwards. ... [I]t is precisely *because* the government could have enacted a wholesale prohibition of the underlying conduct that it is permissible for the government to take the less intrusive step of allowing the conduct, but reducing the demand through restrictions on advertising."[41]

The Court, in taking this position, appears to be adding another dimension to the test of restrictions on commercial speech: whether or not the "underlying conduct that was the subject of the advertising restrictions was constitutionally protected and could not have been prohibited by the State." It would appear that this element becomes a prior question to the four elements announced in *Central Hudson* and would therefore render *Central Hudson* inapplicable in cases involving advertising associated with constitutionally protected conduct. On the other hand, if the underlying conduct is not protected, the state apparently has great latitude in the regulation of advertising about it.

IV. CONCLUSION

In its addition of the notion that it is the underlying conduct that constitutes a primary issue when validity of advertising restriction is being adjudicated, the Supreme Court is introducing a new and potentially quite radical element into the commercial speech debate. Put very simply, if the conduct is constitutionally protected, such as access to contraceptives or abortion, the advertising cannot be banned. However, if the conduct is not constitutionally protected, such as access to casino gambling, the advertising can be banned. The Court made this point clear when it noted the power of the states to regulate "products or activities deemed harmful, such as cigarettes, alcoholic beverages, and prostitution."[42] Thus, for example, although the Supreme Court has had the opportunity to directly examine the first amendment implications

40. 13 MEDIA L. REP 1033, 1041 (1986).
41. *Id.*
42. *Id.*

of regulation of alcoholic beverage advertising twice recently, and on both occasions has refused to do so,[43] after *Posadas* there can be no question of the ability of a state to restrain such commercial speech.

However, what is left unanswered by Chief Justice Rehnquist in *Posadas* is the ability of the state to regulate in the middle ground: the vast majority of advertising in this country is neither for products and services related to constitutionally protected conduct, nor for "products and activities deemed harmful, such as cigarettes, alcoholic beverages, and prostitution." Rather, most advertising is for products and services that fall in the middle of the spectrum. What does *Posadas* say about these sort of advertisements? A strict reading of the case would suggest that a state can regulate and even ban, consistent with the *Central Hudson* test, advertising of a vast array of products and services if such a ban, in the eyes of the state, acts to reduce demand for items the state believes to have a "serious harmful effect on the health, safety and welfare of its citizens." Under this reasoning, could a state ban television commercials for highly sugared products aimed at children? Could commercials for products containing known carcinogens be banned? A number of questions crucially important to both the advertising and legal communities have been raised by *Posadas*, and their answers may well signal the dissolution of the present commercial speech doctrine.

43. A Mississippi law barring most in-state advertising of beer and wine was challenged in *Dunagin v. Oxford* (10 MEDIA L. REP. 1001 [1983]) and was upheld by the Fifth Circuit Court of Appeals. The case was not granted *certiorari* by the Supreme Court, thus leaving the state law intact. In June 1984, the Supreme Court handed down its decision in *Capital Cities Cable v. Crisp* (10 MEDIA L. REP. 1873 [1984]). At issue here was an Oklahoma ban on alcoholic beverage commercials coming into Oklahoma on imported cable television signals. Although the high Court did strike down the ban, it did not do so on first amendment grounds. Rather, it held that Oklahoma's ban was preempted by the Federal Communication Commission's regulations governing cable signal carriage; the ban was in direct conflict with federal law.

ROBERT L. SPELLMAN

The First Amendment Defense to Negligent Misstatement

Robert L. Spellman is the head of the
News-Editorial Sequence at the School of
Journalism of Southern Illinois University
at Carbondale.

More than sixty years ago, New York courts[1] held that readers cannot recover damages from the news media for injuries sustained due to negligent reporting of nondefamatory false information. The common-law holding was adopted throughout the United States. As the Missouri Supreme Court said, "No action for damages lies against a newspaper for merely inaccurate reporting when the publication does not constitute libel."[2] That rule was based on the lack of any contractual or fiduciary relationship between news outlets and news consumers. During the past two decades, reflecting efforts to ease requirements for recovery in tort suits, the rule has been challenged.[3] Now, in an Ohio decision likely to be adopted nationwide, the common-law rule has been reaffirmed and given a constitutional foundation.[4]

The rule is stated in *American Jurisprudence* as:

1. Jaillet v. Cashman, 115 Misc. 383, 189 N.Y.S. 743 (1921), *aff'd*, 202 App. Div. 805, 194 N.Y.S. 947 (1922), *aff'd*, 235 N.Y. 511, 139 N.E. 714 (1923).
2. Lanworthy v. Pulitzer Pub. Co., 368 S.W.2d 385, 390 (Mo. 1963).
3. See, e.g., Gutter v. Dow Jones, Inc., 22 Ohio St.3d (1986); Libertelli v. Hoffman-LaRoche, 7 MEDIA L. REP. 1734 (S.D.N.Y. 1981); Tumminello v. Bergen Evening Record, 454 F. Supp. 1156 (D.N.J. 1978); Demuth Development Corp. v. Merck & Co., Inc., 432 F. Supp. 990 (E.D.N.Y. 1977); Hanberry v. Hearst Corporation, 1 Cal. App.3d 149, 81 Cal. Rptr. 519 (1969); Sacco v. Herald Statesman, Inc., 32 Misc.2d 729, 223 N.Y.S.2d 329 (1961).

    This articles does not discuss cases in which plaintiffs have alleged negligent incitement, e.g., *Olivia N. v. National Broadcasting Company, Inc.*, 126 Cal. App.3d 488, 178 Cal. Rptr. 888 (1981). Often the statements in incitement cases are factually false or are part of fictional portrayals. Plaintiffs generally have been unsuccessful in recovering under an incitement theory. *Contra*: Weirum v. RKO General, Inc., 15 Cal.3d 40, 123 Cal. Rptr. 468, 539 P.2d 36 (1975). See discussion of incitement cases in Hoffman, *From Random House to Mickey Mouse: Liability for Negligent Publishing and Broadcasting*, 21 TORT AND INSURANCE L.J. 65 (Fall 1985).
4. *Gutter, supra* note 3. Annot., 56 ALR4th 1162.

> In the absence of a contract, fiduciary relationship, or inten-
> tional design to cause injury, a newspaper publisher is not
> liable to a member of the public to whom all news is liable
> to be disseminated for a negligent misstatement in an item
> of news, not amounting to libel, published by the publisher,
> unless he wilfully originates or circulates it knowing it to be
> false, and it is calculated to and does, as the proximate cause,
> result in injury to another person.[5]

The landmark New York case arose when Gaston Jaillet, an investor, sued Dow Jones & Co. In March of 1920, Dow Jones carried an inaccurate report on its wire about the effect of a U.S. Supreme Court decision on taxation of dividends. Acting on the report, Jaillet sold stocks instead of holding or buying. The decision proved unprofitable when the stock market rose after accurate information on the Court's decision was received. Jaillet sued and lost.[6] The victory for Dow Jones was affirmed by New York's highest court.[7]

The trial court said there is a "moral obligation upon every one to say nothing that is not true," but the law does not impose a legal duty "unless it constitutes a breach of contract obligation or trust, or amounts to a deceit, libel or slander."[8] Jaillet's action could be sustained, the court commented, only if a news outlet was liable "to every member of the community who was misled by the incorrect report."[9] The court dismissed the suit after finding that Jaillet and Dow Jones had "no contract or fiduciary relationship."[10]

The decision rested on the doctrine of privity. As applied to negligent misstatement, the doctrine holds that damages can be recovered for negligence only if there is a relationship of contract or trust between parties.[11] The doctrine stems from the perception of courts that business firms and individuals should be held responsible only for obligations directly undertaken and not to the public generally. To hold otherwise would impose the "spectre of unlimited liability, with claims devastating in number and amount crushing the defendant because of a momentary lapse."[12]

5. Newspapers, Periodicals & Press Assns., § 22, 58 AM. JUR.2d 148.
6. *Supra* note 1, 189 N.Y.S. at 744.
7. *Supra* note 1, 139 N.E. at 714.
8. *Supra* note 1, 189 N.Y.S. at 744.
9. *Id.*
10. *Id.*
11. *Ultramares Corp. v. Touche*, 255 N.Y. 170, 174 N.E. 441 (1931) (Cardozo, C.J.).
12. W. PROSSER, LAW OF TORTS 708 (4th ed. 1971).

I. POST-*JAILLET* CASES

The New Mexico Supreme Court considered the *Jaillet* rule[13] after the *Albuquerque Journal* published in 1932 a false story saying George Curry, a former governor, had died. Curry's son suffered a heart attack after reading the report and sued for damages. The court said it could find no precedent for allowing recovery of damages and "the existence of such right is not probable, in view of the fact that thousands of similar negligent acts must have occurred in the business of publication of news in this country, and Great Britain and its dependencies, causing grief and worry."[14] The court held that in both the United States and Great Britain the common law "does not recognize, as actionable, injuries resulting from negligently spoken or written words."[15]

In addition to its common-law defense, the *Journal* claimed the first amendment prevented any recovery for injuries from negligent misstatements by the press. But the court said it need not decide to "what extent, if any, the liberty of the press and speech as we understand it is involved."[16]

A Chicago newspaper in 1936 quoted a physician on what he asserted was an effective remedy for dandruff. A reader purchased the remedy and claimed to have suffered severe injuries when she used it. She sued the newspaper.[17] Relying on *Jaillet*, an appellate court upheld a lower court's dismissal of the suit.[18] A similar result was reached in 1944 when a song producer sued the show "Hit Parade." The producer claimed his song was one of the most popular in the country and negligently had been left off the show.[19] A court also dismissed in 1961 a suit in which a businessman claimed he had lost profits after a newspaper negligently and falsely reported that he had been accused of assault.[20]

A small break in the *Jaillet* dike came in 1969 in *Hanberry v. Hearst Corporation*.[21] Zayda Hanberry purchased shoes that had been advertised in *Good Housekeeping* magazine and had received the magazine's "consumers' guaranty." The so-called guaranty stated *Good Housekeeping* was satisfied that products advertised in the magazine "are good ones and that the advertising claims made for them in our magazine are truthful."[22] The shoes had soles that easily slipped on a smooth floor. Hanberry slipped on

13. Curry v. Journal Pub. Co., 68 P.2d 168 (N.M. 1937).
14. *Id.* at 169.
15. *Id.* at 176.
16. *Id.*
17. Mac Kown v. Illinois Publishing & Printing Co., 289 Ill. App. 59, 6 N.E.2d 526 (1937).
18. *Id.* at 529–530.
19. *Advance Music Corp. v. American Tobacco Co.*, 183 Misc. 645, 50 N.Y.S.2d 287 (1944), *aff'd*, 268 App. Div. 707, 53 N.Y.S.2d 337 (1944), *rev'd on other grounds*, 296 N.Y. 79, 70 N.E.2d 401 (1946).
20. *Sacco, supra* note 3.
21. *Supra* note 3.
22. *Supra* note 3, 81 Cal. Rptr. at 521.

her kitchen floor and sustained severe injuries. She sued and alleged negligent misrepresentation.

Conceding that privity did not exist between *Good Housekeeping* and Hanberry, a California appellate court nevertheless allowed the suit to continue.[23] It did so because it was "influenced more by public policy than by whether such cause of action can be comfortably fitted into one of the law's traditional categories of liability."[24] The court said that *Good Housekeeping* had used the so-called guaranty "to enhance the value" of the magazine "as an advertising medium."[25] Further, the magazine allowed advertisers to use the "Consumers' Guaranty Seal" in other media. Thus, the court reasoned, the magazine "voluntarily involved itself in the marketing process" and "loaned its reputation to promote and induce the sale of a given product."[26] As a result, "public policy imposes on it the duty to use ordinary care in issuance of its seal and certification of quality so that members of the consuming public who rely on its endorsement are not unreasonably exposed to the risk of harm."[27]

The court did not discuss *Jaillet* or other cases involving false editorial statements. Instead, it relied on product liability cases for support. As a result *Hanberry* is not good authority for overturning the *Jaillet* rule. At most, it applies only to negligent misstatements in commercial messages, and then only if some type of imprimatur is put on the message. This conclusion is buttressed by *Yuhas v. Mudge*,[28] a New Jersey case. Therein a court found *Popular Mechanics* was not liable to a minor who was injured by fireworks purchased as a result of an advertisement in the magazine.[29] In a *Jaillet*-like statement, the court said to "impose the suggested broad legal duty upon publishers of nationally circulated magazines, newspapers and other publications would not only be impractical or unrealistic, but would have a staggering effect on the commercial world and our economic system."[30] Such liability, the court added, would be "in an indeterminate amount for an indeterminate time to an indeterminate class" and could be justified only if a publication "undertakes to warrant, guarantee or endorse the product."[31] Clearly there is a difference between the endorsement, made after product testing, in *Hanberry* and either advertising or news.

A New York court did not mention *Jaillet* in setting forth a higher standard than negligence in false advertising cases. In *Suarez v. Under-*

23. *Id.*
24. *Id.*
25. *Id.* at 522.
26. *Id.*
27. *Id.*
28. 129 N.J. Super. 207, 322 A.2d 824 (App. Div. 1974).
29. *Id.*, 322 A.2d at 825.
30. *Id.*
31. *Id.*, quoting *Ultramares, supra* note 11.

wood,[32] advertisements for a hair implantation process had been run in *Newsday* in 1978. The process turned out to be hazardous. In 1979, after it had stopped running ads for the process, *Newsday* printed a news story about medical criticism of the process. A hair implant client sued the newspaper for misrepresentation. The suit was dismissed. Where a newspaper does not endorse or warrant a product, the court held, liability can be imposed for false advertising only if there is an intent to harm or the newspaper acts with reckless abandon.[33] The court said that under ordinary circumstances a newspaper has no duty to investigate the effect an ad will have on consumers.[34]

A Florida appellate court, in *Cardozo v. True*,[35] denied recovery to a woman who sued the bookseller who sold her a cookbook. The woman became ill after eating a small slice of a dasheen plant which she had planned to cook according to a recipe in the book. She claimed the book was a defective product because it failed to warn her that uncooked dasheen plants were poisonous. She maintained the bookseller breached an implied warranty under the Uniform Commercial Code and thus was strictly liable for any harm caused. The court said the bookseller only warranted the physical properties of the book and was not liable for the "thoughts and ideas conveyed thereby."[36]

The court said it would violate public policy to require a bookseller "to evaluate the thought processes of the many authors and publishers of the hundreds and often thousands of books which the merchant offers for sale."[37] Further, the court asserted, the U.S. Supreme Court in *Gertz v. Robert Welch, Inc.*,[38] a defamation case, barred courts from imposing strict liability "against one passing on printed words without an opportunity to investigate them."[39] The court avoided any judgment on whether the author of the cookbook could be held liable for on a negligence claim,[40] but it did suggest that it was unlikely a publisher could be found responsible.[41]

A New York court ruled a publisher of a pamphlet on birth control could not be held liable "for all misstatements . . . to a potentially unlimited public for a potentially unlimited period."[42] Planned Parenthood had been sued for negligently misrepresenting in a pamphlet that after a sterilization

---

32. 103 Misc.2d 445, 426 N.Y.S.2d 208 (Queens Co.), *aff'd* 449 N.Y.S. 208 (App. Div. 1981).
33. *Id.*, 426 N.Y.S.2d at 210, quoting *Goldstein v. Garlick*, 318 N.Y.S.2d 370 (Queens Co. 1971).
34. *Id.*
35. 342 So.2d 1053 (Fla. App. 1977).
36. *Id.* at 1056.
37. *Id.*
38. 418 U.S. 323, 94 S. Ct. 2997, 41 L.Ed.2d 789 (1974).
39. *Cardozo, supra* note 35, at 1056.
40. *Id.* at 1057.
41. *Id.* at 1056.
42. Roman v. City of New York, 110 Misc.2d 799, 442 N.Y.S.2d 945, 948 (Queens Co. 1981).

operation, birth control was not necessary to avoid pregnancy. The court noted that the plaintiff's sole relationship with Planned Parenthood was the reading of the pamphlet. Relying on *Jaillet*, the court said such a publisher-reader relationship was insufficient to impose upon Planned Parenthood liability for negligent misrepresentation.[43]

A publisher did lose a negligence action after a junior high school student was injured while performing an experiment set forth in a textbook.[44] No claim of misstatement was made. Rather, damages were sought on a claim of negligent failure to warn of a hazardous aspect of the experiment. A jury awarded the plaintiff $10,000. The publisher did not appeal. Other than the chart cases, discussed below, the case is the only one which could be found in which a publisher was found liable for negligence in the act of publishing.[45] The case is unreported and outside the legal mainstream.

II. THE MARINE AND CHART CASES

Another form of publication liability action has arisen during the past two decades. Both government and private publishers of marine and air charts have been sued when mistakes in charts were alleged to have caused accidents. Recovery has been sought under both negligence and strict liability theories. Only recently have first amendment defenses been raised by private publishers. Such defenses cannot be raised by government agencies.

The United States was sued after a tug's anchor ruptured a natural gas pipeline in Tampa harbor.[46] The rupture caused an explosion and fire. The tug captain had relied upon a chart of Tampa harbor published by the U.S. Coast and Geodetic Survey. The pipeline was not shown on the chart. The lawsuit reached the U.S. Court of Appeals for the Fifth Circuit. The court found the federal government had no liability, but only because the Coast and Geodetic Survey had published a correction prior to the explosion.[47] The court held a duty of prudence was owed by the federal government to shipowners because it knew its charts would be "relied on as accurate portrayals of the waters covered."[48] The court said the charts "are not just casual publications which may be of interest to or fall into hands of an indeterminate number of users."[49] It cited *Jaillet* favorably. However, in doing so, the court said a newspaper's lack of liability for negligent misstatement depended on the absence of "some special relationship between

43. *Id.*
44. *Carter v. Rand McNally & Co.*, No. 76–1864–F (D.Mass. 1980). The case is discussed in 17 TRIAL 89 (1981) and Wallis, *"Negligent Publishing" Implications for University Publishers*, 9 J. COLL. & UNIV. LAW 209 (1982).
45. *Id.*
46. DeBardeleben Marine Corp. v. United States, 451 F.2d 140 (5th Cir. 1971).
47. *Id.* at 149.
48. *Id.* at 148.
49. *Id.*

writer and reader."[50] That special relationship did exist between mariners and the Coast and Geodetic Survey, the court found, due to the federal government's traditional role as chart supplier and its knowledge that the law required mariners to carry accurate charts.[51]

DeBardeleben is unusual only in that the government tried to establish that, in its role as publisher, it had no duty to avoid negligent misstatement. Liability for negligent misstatement has been imposed in other cases involving publication of maps and charts by federal agencies.[52]

In three cases Jeppesen & Co., a publisher of airport approach charts prepared by the Federal Aviation Administration (FAA), was found to have published a defective product. Strict liability was imposed under Section 402A, *Restatement (Second) of Torts*.[53]

Aetna Casualty & Surety Co. v. Jeppesen & Co.[54] stemmed from a 1964 crash of a Bonanza Airlines plane on its approach to a landing at Las Vegas, Nevada. The approach chart was not found to be inaccurate. Rather, it was found defective because two portrayals of the approach were drawn to different scales. The Ninth Circuit Court of Appeals said the "conflict between the information conveyed by words and numbers and the information conveyed by graphics rendered the chart unreasonably dangerous and a defective product."[55] *Saloomey v. Jeppesen & Co.*[56] resulted from the crash of a private plane, piloted by an off-duty airline pilot, at Martinsburg, West Virginia, in 1975. The pilot had no chart for the Martinsburg airport. Instead, he relied on a Washington, DC, area chart which incorrectly indicated that Martinsburg had a full instrument approach landing system. In upholding a lower court verdict of strict liability, the Second Circuit Court of Appeals said, "By publishing and selling the charts, Jeppesen undertook a special responsibility, as seller, to insure that consumers will not be injured by the use of the charts. . . ."[57] A $1.5 million judgment was affirmed.

Jeppesen & Co. was sued in *Brocklesby v. United States*[58] after a World Airways plane crashed in 1973 at Cold Bay, Alaska. The Ninth Circuit Court of Appeals found that Jeppesen & Co., unlike the situations in *Aetna*

---

50. *Id.*
51. *Id.* at 149.
52. Reminga v. United States, 631 F.2d 449 (6th Cir. 1980); Sullivan v. United States, 299 F. Supp. 835 (N.D. Ala. 1968), aff'd 411 F.2d 794 (5th Cir. 1969); Medley v. United States, 541 F. Supp. 1211 (N.D. Cal. 1982); Alnutt v. United States, 498 F. Supp. 832 (W.D. Mo. 1980).
53. Section 402A states: "One who sells any product in a defective condition unreasonably dangerous to the user or consumer or to his property is subject to liability for physical harm thereby caused to the ultimate user or consumer, or to his property. . . ."
54. 642 F.2d 339 (9th Cir. 1981).
55. *Id.* at 342.
56. 707 F.2d 671 (2nd Cir. 1983).
57. *Id.* at 676–677.
58. Brocklesby v. United States, 753 F.2d 794, amended 767 F.2d 1288 (9th Cir. 1985).

and *Saloomey*, had accurately reproduced information for Cold Bay that had been published by the FAA. However, the court said, Jeppesen went beyond mere republication of government regulations. It had produced a product—the chart—which was a graphic portrayal of FAA information. Government information served only as components of the chart.

> If . . . a trade journal had accurately published the government's instrument approach procedure in text form and a pilot had used the procedure as printed in the journal, the journal would be immune from strict liability. . . . Jeppesen's charts are more than just a republication of the text of the government's procedures. Jeppesen converts a government procedure from text into graphic form and represents that the chart contains all necessary information.[59]

The *Brocklesby* court at first rejected a first amendment defense based on commercial speech. The court said the first amendment permits many forms of regulation of commercial speech, including protection of the public from "false or misleading commercial messages."[60] Further, the court continued, requiring "a chart manufacturer to produce a safe product would have no significant chilling effect on freedom of speech."[61] In an amended opinion, the court withdrew its rejection and simply refused to consider any first amendment defenses because they had been raised for the first time on appeal. This included Jeppesen's claim that the first amendment bars imposing of strict liability for published material such as charts.[62] An award of $9.3 million was affirmed.

An Arizona appellate court ruled that Jeppesen could not be held responsible when an accident resulted from the failure of the pilot of an airliner to follow an accurate chart. In *Times-Mirror Co. v. Sisk*,[63] the court said liability cannot be imposed on the publisher of a chart where "there was evidence that the approach as shown on Jeppesen's chart was safe if followed. . . ."[64] Jeppesen challenged the claim that its charts were products within the meaning of Section 402A, *Restatement (Second) of Torts*. The court expressed "serious misgivings about whether this is a products liability case," but avoided ruling on the issue.[65]

The chart cases are troubling. Charts are distributed to large numbers of people. Given the huge number of pilots in the United States, it is

---

59. *Id.*, 767 F.2d at 1297–1298.
60. *Id.*, 753 F.2d at 803.
61. *Id.*
62. *Id.*, 767 F.2d at 1295.
63. 122 Ariz. 174, 593 P.2d 924 (App. 1979).
64. *Id.*, 593 P.2d at 928.
65. *Id.* at 927.

conceptually difficult to distinguish between them and the investors of *Jaillet* or the cookbook users of *Cardozo*. If the cases were distinguished on the basis that *Jaillet*-like information is transmitted by news wires or newspapers, then cookbooks and chemistry textbooks would logically be in the same category as charts. The distinction drawn in *Brocklesby* between mere republication of a federal regulation in a trade journal and using information to create a new information product is unsatisfactory. Much news reporting is taking information from several sources and combining it into a story that provides context and interpretation. To describe the information in a chart—in contrast to its physical properties—as a product and then impose strict liability under product liability law misses the essence. The information is a means of expression. Although it may be perilous to analogize the chart cases with defamation, it appears the strict liability cases violate the constitutional rule of no liability without fault set forth in *Gertz v. Robert Welch, Inc.*[66] Certainly, chart publishers can be expected to raise first amendment defenses more vigorously in future cases. Meanwhile, the chart cases can be viewed as narrow exceptions to the law on negligent misstatement and general circulation publications.

III. THE FIRST AMENDMENT DEFENSE EMERGES

The first amendment is the cornerstone of three recent federal district court decisioons on negligent misstatement. Two involve publication of technical information. The third stemmed from newspaper crime reporting.

Demuth Development Corporation manufactured a vaporizer that used a chemical listed in *The Merck Index*, an encyclopedia of chemicals and drugs. The Index listed more than 10,000 chemicals and drugs and had sold about 276,500 copies prior to mid-1974. The index incorrectly said the chemical used in DeMuth's vaporizer was toxic. Demuth claimed the index description caused it to lose customers and sued for $4 million in damages.[67] A federal district court refused to overturn the *Jaillet* rule and went further. It held that "Merck's right to publish free of fear of liability is guaranteed by the First Amendment. . . . and the overriding societal interest in the untrammeled dissemination of knowledge."[68] The decision marked the first time a court used the first amendment to reject a claim of negligent misstatement against a publisher.

The difficulty with the *Demuth* court's first amendment holding was its reliance for Supreme Court authority on *dictum* in *Gertz v. Robert Welch, Inc.*[69] The *dictum* said that "(a)lthough the erroneous statement of fact is not worthy of constitutional protection, it is nevertheless inevitable in free

66. *Supra* note 38.
67. *Demuth, supra* note 3, at 990–991.
68. *Id.* at 993.
69. *Supra* note 38.

debate. . . . And punishment of error runs the risk of inducing a cautious and restrictive exercise of the constitutionally guaranteed freedoms of speech and press."[70] The *dictum* does not support a finding of constitutional protection against liability for negligent misstatement. In fact, *Gertz* permits states to impose liability for negligent false and defamatory statements.[71]

Unlike *Demuth*, where the plaintiff was a manufacturer, the plaintiff in *Libertelli v. Hoffman-LaRoche*[72] was a consumer. Barbara Libertelli's doctor prescribed the use of Valium, a drug manufactured by Hoffman-LaRoche. She used it for four years and became addicted. She named Medical Economics Co., publisher of the *Physicians Desk Reference*, as a defendant in her suit, and claimed her doctor had relied on the reference book in prescribing Valium. She maintained the publisher was grossly negligent for not including a warning of the drug's addictive nature in its information on Valium in *Physicians Desk Reference*. She claimed Medical Economics should have conducted independent tests rather than simply printing information on the drug supplied by Hoffman-LaRoche. There was a statement in the reference book that product information was supplied by manufacturers and the publisher did not advocate use of any product.

The court dismissed the claim on the basis of New York common law and because it offended the first amendment. Under New York law, the court said, liability cannot be imposed on a publisher of product information unless it warrants the product or acts with recklessness or intent to harm.[73] Unlike the *Demuth* court, which used *Gertz* as its first amendment authority, the court relied on *Time, Inc. v. Hill*.[74] The court held a publisher of an information article of public interest cannot be held liable for an error unless the article was published with knowledge it was false or with reckless disregard for the truth.[75] Under *Time, Inc. v. Hill*, a finding is necessary that the information in the article was a matter of public interest. The court said information about "medical matters is sufficiently important to the public interest" to warrant the imposition of the standard of knowing falsity or reckless disregard of the truth.[76] One difficulty with the case is that it is unreported and therefore not the best authority.

Salvatore Tumminello was under indictment in New Jersey for murder. The *Bergen Evening Record* printed an inaccurate report that a five-year statute of limitations applied to murder. If the report had been accurate, the indictment would have been dismissed. Claiming he had been plunged into despondency when he learned the statute did not apply to murder, Tum-

70. *Id.*, 418 U.S. at 340.
71. *Id.* at 347.
72. *Supra* note 3.
73. *Id.* at 1735.
74. 385 U.S. 374, 87 S. Ct. 534, 17 L.Ed.2d 456 (1967). Richard M. Nixon was attorney for Hill.
75. *Libertelli, supra* note 3, at 1736.
76. *Id.*

minello sued the newspaper for negligent misstatement.[77] While the suit could be termed frivolous and was dismissed,[78] the court, as did the one in *Libertelli* and unlike the one in *Demuth*, relied on *Time, Inc. v. Hill.*

In *Hill*, an article about a Broadway play was published in *Life* magazine. The play was a dramatization about a family that had been held hostage by escaped convicts. Part of the dramatization was an inaccurate portrayal, and the inaccuracies were contained in the *Life* article. Hill sued for invasion of privacy. The Supreme Court reversed a state court's verdict in favor of Hill.[79] In doing so, the Court held that damages could be recovered for false reports of newsworthy matters only if they were published with knowing falsity or with serious doubts as to their truth or falsity.[80]

The *Tumminello* decision did not cite (nor did *Libertelli*) the parts of *Hill* upon which it relied, but two passages are particularly important. In one the Court held that liability could not be imposed for "false reports of matters of public interest in the absence of proof that the defendant published the report with knowledge of its falsity or in reckless disregard of the truth."[81] In the other, the Court said:

> We create a grave risk of serious impairment of the indispensable service of a free press in a free society if we saddle the press with the impossible burden of verifying to a certainty the facts associated in news articles . . . particularly as related to nondefamatory matter. Even negligence would be a most elusive standard, especially when the content of the speech itself affords no warning of prospective harm to another through falsity. A negligence test would place on the press the intolerable burden of guessing how a jury might assess the reasonableness of steps taken by it to verify. . . .[82]

In *Tumminello*, the court simply said that "New Jersey *could not*, consistent with the requirements of the First Amendment, impose liability for a negligently untruthful news story."[83]

IV. THE INVESTOR AND THE *JOURNAL*

In May of 1983, a case arose in Ohio which came exceptionally close to duplicating the events that had produced *Jaillet* more than sixty years

---

77. *Tumminello, supra* note 3, at 1157, 1159.
78. *Id.* at 1160.
79. *Supra* note 74, 385 U.S. at 398.
80. 385 U.S. at 388.
81. *Id.*
82. 385 U.S. at 389.
83. *Tumminello, supra* note 3, at 1159.

before. Phil Gutter, an investor, purchased bonds that the *Wall Street Journal* inaccurately had reported were trading with interest. After the newspaper corrected the report, Gutter sold his bonds at a loss of $1,693. He sued the newspaper for negligent misstatement. His suit was dismissed by a lower court. An appellate court reversed and ruled Gutter should have the opportunity to prove that he was a member of a class of traders whose reliance on the bond information could have been foreseen by the *Wall Street Journal*.[84]

The court was persuaded of the newspaper's potential liability by Ohio's adoption of the modern common-law rule on negligent misstatement. As set forth in *Restatement (Second) of Torts*, an authority widely accepted by courts, the rule says:

> One who, in the course of his business, profession or employment, or in any other transaction in which he has a pecuniary interest, supplies false information for the guidance of others in their business transactions, is subject to liability for pecuniary loss caused to them by their justifiable reliance upon the information, if he fails to exercise reasonable care or competence in obtaining or communicating the information.[85]

The *Restatement* says that only "a limited group of persons" whom a person "intends the information to influence" can recover damages.[86] The rule was not intended to impose liability to newspaper readers generally. One of the *Restatement*'s examples, obviously taken from *Mac Kown*, states:

> The A Newspaper negligently publishes in one of its columns a statement that a certain proprietary drug is a sure cure for dandruff. B, who is plagued with dandruff, reads the statement and in reliance upon it purchases a quantity of the drug. It proves worthless as a dandruff cure and B suffers pecuniary loss. The A Newspaper is not liable to B.[87]

The Ohio court agreed that the *Wall Street Journal* was not liable to all its readers, but it said Gutter might be able to prove he was part of a "special, limited class whose reliance upon the information is specifically foreseen."[88] The court noted that the *De Bardeleban* decision left open the possibility of liability where there was "some special relationship between

84. Gutter v. Dow Jones, Inc., slip op., No. 84AP–1029 (Franklin Co. Ct. of App., May 10, 1985).
85. Section 552.
86. Section 552.
87. Section 552, comment c.
88. *Gutter, supra* note 84, slip op. at 7.

the writer and reader."[89] The holding in *Jaillet* was rejected because Jaillet "was found to be a member of the general public in relation to the supplier of information, rather than a member of a limited class whose reliance upon the information was foreseen."[90] The court believed Gutter might prove that the *Wall Street Journal* knew and could foresee that bond investors as a class relied on bond tables in their trading. The court said *Hill* was an invasion-of-privacy action and therefore not germane. It asserted "no First Amendment right is involved."[91]

Holding that "important First Amendment interests are involved in news accounts,"[92] the Ohio Supreme Court reversed. "Accuracy in news reporting is certainly a desideratum," the court remarked, "but the chilling effect of imposing a high duty of care on those in the business of news dissemination and making that duty run to a wide range of readers or TV viewers would have a chilling effect which is unacceptable under our Constitution."[93] The court conceded that Gutter might be able to prove that the *Wall Street Journal* was negligent, but it questioned whether reliance on a news account for bond trading information could be considered "justifiable."[94] To rule otherwise, the court commented, "would in effect extend liability to all the world."[95] The court based its decision on both common-law public policy and the first amendment, saying "the competing public policy and constitutional concerns tilt decidedly in favor of the press when mere negligence is alleged."[96]

The court traced its common-law rejection of negligent misstatement liability for the news media to *Jaillet*.[97] Not so clear were the roots of its first amendment holding. The court cited both *Tumminello*, which relied on *Hill*, and *Demuth*, which relied on *Gertz*.[98] Most likely the court was convinced by the holding in *Hill*. Attorneys for both the *Wall Street Journal* and Gutter argued the significance of *Hill* in their briefs to the court.[99] Further, the court said *Demuth* was a progeny of *Jaillet*, suggesting it considered *Demuth* primarily a common-law decision.[100] In any event, because *Tumminello* was cited as authority, the Supreme Court's reasoning in *Hill* is part of the first amendment foundation of *Gutter*.

89. *Id.*
90. *Id.* at 6.
91. *Id.* at 5.
92. *Gutter, supra* note 3, 22 Ohio St.3d at 289.
93. *Id.*, quoting *Tumminello*.
94. *Id.*
95. *Id.*
96. *Id.* at 291.
97. *Id.* at 290.
98. *Id.* at 289–290.
99. Gutter v. Dow Jones, Ohio Supreme Court, Memorandum in Support of Jurisdiction, July 12, 1985, and Memorandum of Plaintiff-Appellee Opposing Jurisdiction, Aug. 12, 1985.
100. 22 Ohio St.3d at 290.

V. CONCLUSIONS

The past two decades have seen a huge expansion of tort liability by American courts. The press has not escaped the probings of lawyers seeking to expand the outer boundaries of tort law. In marine and air chart cases, the boundaries have been pushed outward. There is a possibility that the chart cases will not remain a narrow exception to the law on publishing and misstatement. There may be a spill-over into others areas of technical and scientific publication. However, so far courts have not considered strong first amendment defenses in chart cases, and there may be a contraction rather than expansion of liability.

Generally, however, courts have refused to impose liability on the news media for negligent, false nondefamatory statements. Had they done so, the consequences would have been severe in an era that has seen an expansion of both business and consumer reporting.[101] Readers do rely on the news media. The Ohio Supreme Court's decision, based as it is on firm constitutional footings, likely will be followed by other state and federal courts. The decision's primary significance is its reliance on the first amendment. The winds of change are sweeping aside common-law tort concepts. The constitutional foundation should protect the immunity of the news media for negligent misstatement from being swept aside.

101. Attorneys for the *Journal* in *Gutter* suggested that imposition of liability in financial reporting could lead to suits over false weather reports, television and movie listings, recipes, marriage, birth and death notices, personal advice and advertisements. *Supra* note 99. Memorandum in Support of Jurisdiction.

DAVID D. VESTAL

The Tobacco Advertising Debate: A First Amendment Perspective

David D. Vestal is a member of the Iowa bar.

On February 18, 1987, Rep. Mike Synar (D-Okla.) introduced a bill in the U.S. House of Representatives imposing a blanket ban on tobacco advertising and promotion.[1] The proposal would extend the present advertising prohibition in the broadcast media to the print media and to other means of promoting tobacco products. The bill was originally given little chance of passage, since an identical bill, introduced in June 1986, was never voted out of committee in the 99th Congress.[2] But there have been dramatic developments in the last two years which have shifted the momentum towards an advertising ban.

First, and most importantly, on July 1, 1986, the Supreme Court decided the case of *Posadas de Puerto Rico Assocs. v. Tourism Co. of Puerto Rico*,[3] which cast serious doubt on a first amendment impediment to the proposed ban. Second, Surgeon General C. Everett Koop told a House subcommittee in August of 1986 that he personally supported legislation that would totally ban the advertising and promotion of tobacco products.[4] Finally, on June 13, 1988, a New Jersey federal jury found Liggett Group, Inc. partly to blame for the 1984 death of smoker Rose Cipollone, concluding that the company failed to warn of the health risks of smoking before warning labels were

---

1. The "Health Protection Act of 1987" would prohibit all tobacco advertisements in newspapers, magazines, and on billboards. The bill would also bar tobacco manufacturers from offering free samples and from sponsoring athletic, artistic, or other events under the registered brand name of a tobacco product. This would prohibit such events as the annual Kool Jazz Festival and the Virginia Slims tennis tournaments. Green, Cigarettes, Reuters, Ltd., Feb. 18, 1987, at 1.
2. Abramson, *Battle Lines Drawn in Cigarette Ad Fight,* Legal Times, Nov. 10, 1986, at 1.
3. 106 S. Ct. 2968 (1986).
4. Tye, *Cigarette Ads Reveal a History of Deceit,* Wall St. J., Aug. 5, 1986, at 27, col. 1.

required in 1966.[5] Considerable evidence was introduced at the trial to suggest that tobacco companies have engaged in misleading advertising.[6]

Between these three events, public sentiment has now begun to shift in favor of an advertising ban. The Synar bill has twice as many co-sponsors in the House as the 1986 version, and even ban opponent James Kilpatrick has been forced to admit that "given the mounting pressure, (Synar's bill) may in fact pass."[7]

The purpose of this article is to evaluate the Synar bill in light of the current first amendment protections afforded commercial speech. This article will address the first amendment issues by tracing the development and theoretical underpinnings of the commercial speech doctrine and analyzing the landmark *Posadas* decision and its application to the Synar proposal. Testing the proposed ban against current doctrine, this article concludes that the Synar bill would pass constitutional muster under *Posadas*. Nonetheless, the Supreme Court should return to the analytically correct position it took in the first commercial speech case, *Valentine v. Chrestensen*[8] in 1942, and announce that commercial speech, including tobacco advertising, lies outside the protection of the first amendment.

I. A BRIEF HISTORY OF TOBACCO ADVERTISING REGULATION

Government intervention in the $22 billion-a-year tobacco marketplace was a direct response to medical evidence linking smoking and cancer.[9] In 1964, Surgeon General Luther L. Terry reported that cigarettes were "a health hazard of sufficient importance . . . to warrant appropriate remedial action." That same year, the Federal Trade Commission proposed that cigarette advertisements carry a printed warning.[10]

The following year Congress preempted the regulatory field, passing a bill requiring cigarette packages carry the warning: "Caution: Cigarette

---

5. Wakin, *Jury: Tobacco Company Liable in Death,* Charlotte Observer, June 14, 1988, at 1, col. 1.
6. Janson, *End to Suit Denied in Smoking Death,* N.Y. Times, April 22, 1988, at 1, col. 1.
7. Kilpatrick, *Smokers and Puritans,* Washington Post, March 3, 1987, at A23, col. 1. Rep. Henry Waxman (D.-Cal.), a chief sponsor of the Synar bill, commented shortly after the bill was introduced that "public opinion on this issue has changed more rapidly than on any other issue I've been associated with. A clear majority of people believe this is the prudent decision." Colford, *Tobacco Ad Foes Press Fight,* Ad. Age, Feb. 23, 1987, at 12.
8. 316 U.S. 52 (1942).
9. Schneider, Klein & Murphy, *Government Regulation of Cigarette Health Information,* 24 J. L. & Econ. 575, 575–76 (1981).
10. Garrison, *Should All Cigarette Advertising Be Banned? A First Amendment and Public Policy Issue,* 25 Am. Bus. L.J. 169, 173 (1987).

Smoking May Be Hazardous To Your Health." The bill excluded warnings on advertisements.[11]

The 1965 Act did not prevent the Federal Communications Commission from regulating broadcast advertising, and in 1967 the FCC instituted a policy requiring broadcasters to air antismoking commercials in response to the cigarette commercials under the "fairness doctrine."[12]

Two years later, in 1969, the FCC proposed a ban on all cigarette advertising in the broadcast media.[13] In direct response to the FCC proposal, Congress passed the Public Health Cigarette Smoking Act of 1969, which banned all cigarette advertising on television and radio as of January 1, 1971.[14]

Congress also changed the required notice on packages to: "Warning: The Surgeon General Has Determined That Cigarette Smoking Is Dangerous To Your Health."

The FTC was eventually successful in forcing the tobacco industry to include warnings on cigarette advertisements. Warnings identical to the package warnings were imposed under the terms of a 1972 consent order.

In 1976, the FTC undertook a comprehensive investigation of cigarette advertising. Based on the results of this investigation, and after a three-year battle, Congress passed the Smoking Prevention Health and Education Act of 1983.[15] The Act strengthened warning labels and required that they be included in all cigarette advertising. The warnings, to be rotated periodically, were made 50 percent larger than before, and were strengthened in tone, warning that cigarette smoke contains carbon monoxide, causes lung cancer,

---

11. *Id.*
12. *Id.* By 1969, tobacco companies were particularly eager to get their ads off the air. In 1967, a court decision had mandated that, under the fairness doctrine, the television networks carry antismoking ads if they carried cigarette ads. Tobacco company executives were so alarmed by the antismoking ads that they banded together and voluntarily agreed to pull their ads off the air, even before Congress acted to ban the ads. Blum, *The Great Tobacco Ad Ban Debate,* Quill 17, 26 (Dec. 1986).
13. The FCC required television and radio stations to air antismoking commercials in a ratio of one antismoking commercial to every four cigarette commercials. Schneider, Klein & Murphy, *supra* note 9, at 576.
14. *Id.* The Public Health Cigarette Smoking Act of 1969, 15 U.S.C. §§1331–1341 (1982) bans cigarette advertising on electronic media. The Act, as amended, now reads: "After January 1, 1971, it shall be unlawful to advertise cigarettes on any medium of electronic communications subject to the jurisdiction of the Federal Communications Commission."
15. After a three-year battle, Congress approved legislation strengthening cigarette warning labels and requiring that they be included in cigarette advertising. The legislation required four new labels warning that cigarette smoke contains carbon monoxide, causes lung cancer, heart disease, and emphysema, and poses significant health risks to pregnant women. The new labels, which are rotated periodically, are 50 percent larger than previous labels. Rovner, *Then to Now: The Cigarette Warning,* Cong. Q. 3051 (Dec. 13, 1986).

heart disease, and emphysema, and poses significant health risks to pregnant women.

To summarize, present governmental policy toward cigarette advertising reflects a combination of warnings designed to inform consumers of the health risks of smoking coupled with a ban on advertising in the broadcast media. Having reviewed current governmental policy, the remainder of the article will focus on the first amendment implications of the proposed changes in that policy.

II. THE PATERNALISM DEBATE

First amendment theorists have long recognized the essential role of speech in cultural and social development. In 1859, John Stuart Mill wrote:

> The peculiar evil of silencing the expression of an opinion is, that it is robbing the human race; posterity as well as the existing generation; those who dissent from the opinion, still more than those who hold it. If the opinion is right, they are deprived of the opportunity of exchanging error for truth: if wrong, they lose, what is almost as great a benefit, the clearer perception and livelier impression of truth, produced by its collision with error.[16]

Justice Holmes took up this theme and translated it into the marketplace of ideas concept. The value of a marketplace of ideas, according to Holmes, lies in the promotion of truth through the collision and free exchange of opinions.[17]

In the commercial speech context, ban opponents have argued that one advantage of counteradvertising over an advertising ban is its appeal to the first amendment tradition of shouting down inaccurate information rather than suppressing it.[18]

16. J. MILL, ON LIBERTY 24 (Oxford Univ. ed. 1971) (1st ed. London 1859).
17. Abrams v. United States, 250 U.S. 616, 630 (1919) (Holmes, J., dissenting).
18. Justice Stevens embraced this tradition in his concurrence in *Central Hudson Gas & Elec. Co. v. Public Serv. Comm.*, wherein he quoted the earlier words of Justice Brandeis:

> To courageous, self-reliant men, with confidence in the power of free and fearless reasoning applied through the processes of popular government, no danger flowing from speech can be deemed clear and present, unless the incidence of the evil apprehended is so imminent that it may befall before there is opportunity for full discussion. If there be time to expose through discussion the falsehood and fallacies, to avert the evil by the processes of education, the remedy to be applied is more speech, not enforced silence.

447 U.S. 557, 582 (1980) (Stevens, J., concurring) (quoting from Whitney v. California, 274 U.S. 357, 376–77 (1927)) (Brandeis, J., concurring).

Ban opponents decry what they label "paternalistic arguments based on the benefits of public ignorance,"[19] and point out that in the past, the Supreme Court has refused to allow legislatures to further their policies by keeping the public ignorant of truthful information concerning lawful commercial activities. As noted first amendment attorney Floyd Abrams put the argument, "in this country we don't strike out at speech to deal with social problems. We try to persuade people with more speech."[20]

Opponents of a tobacco advertising ban draw support from the 1976 Supreme Court case of *Virginia State Board of Pharmacy v. Virginia Consumer Council,* wherein the Court announced that the first amendment protects advertising because purely commercial speech contributes to enlightened public decision-making in a democracy.[21] Pointing out that the proper allocation of resources in a free market economy requires information, the Court concluded from this that the marketplace of ideas theory applies as forcefully to the actual marketplace as it does to political and social theory.[22]

Critics of commercial speech regulation have vehemently argued that governments should not control the content of commercial information reaching the public, suggesting that as long as a product is legal, there should be a right to advertise it. As one ban critic has phrased the argument, "If products of any kind are dangerous to the public, it is the product—not speech about the product—that should be banned."[23]

Applying this argument specifically to the Synar bill, critics have suggested it tries to "discourage sales through a kind of thought control."[24] According to opponents, the Synar bill is based on the premise that consumers cannot be trusted to make intelligent decisions in regard to their personal behavior.

Those favoring a tobacco advertising ban, and in particular the Synar bill, respond that the marketplace of ideas justification is inapplicable in the area of commercial speech because tobacco advertising is not "speech" in the same sense as political commentary or social discussion, and is in fact "remarkable for its insignificance."[25]

19. Maute, *Scrutinizing Lawyer Advertising and Solicitation Rules Under Commercial Speech and Anti-Trust Doctrine,* 13 Hastings Const. L.Q. 487, 499 (1986).
20. Savage, *ABA Refuses to Back Ban on Cigarette Advertising,* L.A. Times, Feb. 17, 1987, at 15, col. 1.
21. 425 U.S. 748, 765 (1976).
22. *Id.*
23. *Ads Have First Amendment Rights,* N.Y. Times, Jan. 9, 1986, at 22, col. 1.
24. Scheibla, *Not Just Blowing Smoke,* Ad. Age, March 2, 1987, at 11. Guy L. Smith IV, vice president for corporate affairs, Philip Morris U.S.A., criticizing the Synar bill, stated, "Pravda does not carry cigarette advertising, or indeed any advertising. Government control of information is typical of totalitarian regimes and dictatorships. Those who favor such a ban hope to control the behavior of Americans by limiting their access to information. Ad bans represent censorship and idea control." N.Y. Times, Dec. 20, 1987, at 7, col. 1.
25. Jackson & Jeffries, *Commercial Speech: Economic Due Process and the First Amendment,* 65 Va. L. Rev. 1, 14 (1979).

Cigarette advertising is unquestionably dominated by "image advertising," portraying smoking as a healthy activity and employing images of young people engaged in sports and physically demanding activities.[26] For the most part cigarette advertisements "try not to deal with tobacco and health issues per se but with ambiguous images relating to health and vitality," according to David G. Altman, a researcher at Stanford University who has studied the history of American cigarette advertising.[27]

Researcher Altman found that about 30 percent of the tobacco ads in magazines feature themes of risk and adventure. "In the face of increasing public knowledge about the risks of smoking and the shrinking of the population of potential smokers, the industry has misrepresented smoking as associated with sex, fun and frolic," Altman concluded.[28]

Simply put, the argument is that, even if the first amendment protects the free interchange of even unpleasant ideas, cigarette advertising is less integrally involved with ideas, does not add information to the public domain, and therefore lies outside the realm of first amendment protection.[29]

The argument that commercial speech bears no relation to the marketplace of ideas and therefore should not be protected is compelling. The value of commercial speech is its usefulness in assisting consumers decide when and from whom to purchase products or services. Thus, the value of commercial speech is in continuing the free market economy, not in enhancing the marketplace of ideas. Commercial speech, in this case tobacco advertising, does not deserve first amendment protection on the grounds that it is equivalent to political debate. To the extent that the *Virginia Pharmacy* case found to the contrary, it was wrongly decided and should be overturned.

The Supreme Court has already retreated from the dubious notion that

---

26. *E.g., supra* note 4.
27. Rothenberg, *Understanding the Dream World of Cigarette Ads,* N.Y. Times, April 24, 1988, at 6E, col. 1.
28. *Id.*
29. *See, e.g.,* Sharpe, *Commercial Expression and the Charter,* 37 U. Toronto L.J. 229, 233 (1987). Distinguishing commercials which deserve first amendment protection from those that do not is problematic. Nonetheless, it can be done. For instance, economists have differentiated between "informative" and "persuasive" advertising. Although all advertising is a combination of information and persuasion, advertising that is primarily persuasive is characterized by nonrational or emotional appeals to consumers. The purpose of persuasive advertising is to differentiate the product from similar brands and thereby create brand loyalty among consumers.

Competition in the tobacco market has been dominated by persuasive advertising and product differentiation. Image creation has played a conspicuous role in brand success. Garrison, *Should All Cigarette Advertising Be Banned?,* 25 Am. Bus. L.J. 169, 182 (1987).

Likewise, the FCC, in its 1974 fairness doctrine report, stated, "We believe that standard product commercials, such as the old cigarette ads, make no meaningful contribution toward informing the public on any side of any issue." The FCC announced that in the future it would only apply the fairness doctrine to commercials "devoted in an obvious and meaningful way to the discussion of public issues." 48 F.C.C.2d 1, 26 (1974). Standards do exist, and workable lines can be drawn.

commercial speech deserves first amendment protection because it enhances the marketplace of ideas. In *Posadas,* the Court, per Justice Rehnquist, for the first time upheld a ban on truthful advertising of a legal product. To be consistent with *Virginia Pharmacy,* the Court should have held that the commercial speech in question, casino advertisements, had value in the marketplace of ideas and therefore was protected from state regulation. Instead, the Court upheld the curtailment of commercial speech, failing to even mention the marketplace enhancement argument which was central to *Virginia Pharmacy* a decade earlier. Therefore, *Posadas* leaves little room for an argument that commercial speech deserves first amendment protection because it enhances public debate.

III. THE REGULATION OF MISLEADING SPEECH

Those on both sides of a tobacco advertising ban agree that, as the Supreme Court has repeatedly held, commercial speech that is misleading is not protected by the first amendment. The rationale for this has always been that since deceptive advertising serves no useful purpose and has such potentially harmful consequences, it can be regulated or even prohibited without violating the first amendment. On this basis, the FTC has been given wide discretion to pursue deceptive advertising.[30]

The two sides diverge on the question of whether tobacco advertising is *per se* misleading. Proponents of an advertising ban argue that tobacco advertising, with total expenditures of nearly $2.5 billion annually,[31] is by its very nature misleading, and thus deserves no first amendment protection whatsoever.[32]

New evidence recently came to light about the misleading nature of tobacco advertising. In the Rose Cipollone trial, for the first time, plaintiffs' lawyers obtained court permission to search the confidential files of the defendant companies and of industry organizations. Scores of internal documents obtained in the search were offered as evidence of a conspiracy by the companies to conceal the dangers of smoking.

Although the jury rejected the conspiracy theory, there was, according to the judge, evidence that the tobacco industry entered into a "sophisticated conspiracy . . . organized to refute, undermine and neutralize information coming from the scientific and medical community and, at the same time, to

---

30. Younger, *Alcoholic Beverage Advertising on the Airwaves,* 34 U.C.L.A. L. Rᴇᴠ. 1139, 1151 (1987).
31. Rothenberg, *supra* note 27, at 6E, col. 1.
32. Garrison, *supra* note 29, at 172.

confuse and mislead the consuming public in an effort to encourage existing smokers to continue and new persons to commence smoking."[33]

Tobacco advertising proponents respond to these charges in three ways. First, they uniformly deny that their advertisements are aimed at minors, insisting that they are instead aimed at getting people who already smoke to switch brands.[34] Second, they argue that ads should not be deemed deceptive just because they are one-sided and incomplete. That is, after all, the nature of all advertising. Government regulation should be directed, they contend, at fraudulent advertising, "not the techniques of image creation present in advertising most products."[35] Third, they are now focusing more than ever before on the public's right to the information contained in tobacco advertising. The argument here is that although tobacco advertisements are primarily persuasive, they are in part informational, for instance, alerting the public to the benefits of low tar and nicotine cigarettes. In addition, all advertisements include the required warnings "and thus convey useful information to consumers."[36]

Although tobacco advertisements do not merit first amendment protection based on their informational content, neither are they so inherently misleading as to be subject to FTC prohibition on that basis. If tobacco advertising is to be banned, the prohibition should be based on a well-considered debate of traditional first amendment principles, and not be imposed through administrative subterfuge. If the government wants to achieve certain supposed beneficial results, it should do so through free and open debate, not by using a restriction on speech to implement hidden policy decisions.

IV. AVOIDING THE SLIPPERY SLOPE

Prior to *Posadas,* commercial speech was afforded significant protection. Although the Court permitted regulations to assure that commercial

---

33. Janson, *supra* note 6, at 1, col. 1. In addition, some contend that tobacco advertising is deceptive because it targets children, and children cannot make informed decisions regarding smoking. In fact, one new focus of ban supporters is contending that tobacco advertising is targeted at minors, and arguing that since sales to minors are generally illegal, the advertisements should be prohibited. Colford, *Tobacco Ad Ban Fails to Win New Support,* Ad. Age, Aug. 3, 1987, at 55.
34. Bloede, *Smoked Out; Counsel Quitting Over Ad Ban Issue,* Ad. Age, May 11, 1987, at 104.
35. Schoeman, *The First Amendment and Restrictions on Advertising of Securities Under the Securities Act of 1933,* Bus. Law 386 (Feb. 1986).
36. Tanner, FTC Chairman Urges Press to Note Threats to Economic Freedoms, AP Wire, Oct. 27, 1987, at 1.

speech was not deceptive,[37] it rejected government attempts to ban truthful commercial speech to achieve nonspeech related objectives. Then the *Posadas* Court upheld a Puerto Rican law restricting advertising of casino gambling, even though gambling is legal there. The Court's 5–4 ruling allowed that if it would be constitutional for a state to prohibit the sale of a product "deemed harmful," it would also be constitutional to prohibit advertising of that product without actually making sale of the product illegal.[38] Although it was *dicta*, the Court for the first time approved a total ban on truthful advertising for a legal product.

If a colorable first amendment basis could be found for banning tobacco advertising, ban opponents argue, there is no reason to believe that the speech regulation would stop there. A tobacco advertising ban has "no precedent and no limiting principle."[39] According to advertising ban foe Floyd Abrams, "censorship is contagious and habit-forming."[40] Others claim that speech regulation, once commenced, "takes on a life of its own,"[41] and that any advertising ban would have "a precedential effect for all other lawful products that are said to do harm."[42] If the current target is tobacco, say ban opponents, "next year it could be beer and wine, red meat or eggs."[43]

Simply stated, ban opponents argue that as long as a product is legal there should be an absolute right to advertise it, assuming the advertising is truthful and nondeceptive. It is not the government's place to dictate advertising content when legal products are involved, so the argument goes, and at least before *Posadas* the Supreme Court position had been to disapprove a blanket ban on commercial speech unless the expression itself was either deceptive or related to unlawful activity.

Ban proponents counter by focusing on what they perceive to be the unique features of tobacco, describing it as the only product which is dangerous to health when used precisely as directed. According to ban proponent and New York lawyer Henry G. Miller, a ban on tobacco advertising will not lead down the slippery slope to prohibiting other forms of advertising as

37. The rationale used by the *Virginia Pharmacy* Court to regulate deceptive commercial speech was that, even though it is protected by the first amendment, it is "heartier" than political speech, and thus can stand up under all the punishment. This position has come under considerable attack. *See, e.g.,* Whelan, *Common Sense and Commercial Speech,* 48 U. PITT. L. REV. 1121, 1132 (1987).
38. Savage, *Harmful Products Ruling Could Halt Tobacco Ads,* L.A. Times, July 2, 1986, at 10, col. 1. According to one recent article, given the Court's treatment of the subject, *Posadas* "may well signal the dissolution of the present commercial speech doctrine." Trauth and Huffman, *The Commercial Speech Doctrine: Posadas Revisionism,* 10:1 COM. & LAW 43, 56 (Feb. 1988).
39. Blum, *supra* note 12, at 31.
40. Savage, *supra* note 20, at 15.
41. Mintz, *Tobacco Press Kit Ignites Controversy,* Wash. Post, Dec. 20, 1987, at K2, col. 4.
42. Colford, *Tobacco Ad Foes Press Fight,* Ad. Age, Feb. 23, 1987, at 12.
43. Marcus, *Clearing the Smoke in New Orleans,* Wash. Post, Feb. 16, 1987, at C2, coi. 1.

well. "Tobacco is a unique danger. To say we cannot distinguish between tobacco and other products is absurd. It's the difference between the bubonic plague and the common cold."[44]

The argument that a prohibition on tobacco advertising would not invite more speech restrictions is incredible. Indeed, it is difficult to see how any principled first amendment distinction can be made between speech about various consumer goods. Either all speech about legal products should be protected or none of it should be. The only problem is that the Court, having come to this conclusion in *Virginia Pharmacy,* made the wrong decision, choosing to afford all commercial speech some protection.

V. DEBATING THE EFFICACY OF AN ADVERTISING BAN

In *Central Hudson* the Court announced a four-part test which has become "the primary standard for commercial speech analysis under the first amendment."[45] The test, set out in the margin,[46] is a framework under which even truthful promotions of lawful products may constitutionally be restricted, so long as the government has a substantial interest in doing so and the restriction directly advances that interest in a manner that is no more extensive than necessary.

Posadas implicitly holds that an advertising restriction must still satisfy the *Central Hudson* test even if the government interest is substantial enough to justify a product ban. Therefore, the Synar bill will survive first amendment challenge only if it can pass the four-part *Central Hudson* test.

Since cigarette advertising involves the promotion of a lawful product and is not inherently misleading, the first element of the *Central Hudson* test would be satisfied. Similarly, it is beyond dispute that the second element of the test would be satisfied, because the government interest in minimizing the adverse health effects of smoking represents a substantial state interest.

The third prong of *Central Hudson* demands a direct connection between the means employed by the state and the interest the state seeks to advance. The Court has rejected advertising bans where the link has been too tenuous. For instance, in *Virginia Pharmacy* the Court found that the government interest was only indirectly furthered by the suppression of commercial

---

44. *Id.*
45. Nienow, *The Common Sense Distinction Between Commercial and Noncommercial Speech,* 14 HASTINGS CONST. L.Q. 869, 878 (1987).
46. For commercial speech to be protected: (1) the advertising must concern a lawful activity and not be misleading; if it satisfies the first prong, the government may restrict advertising only if (2) the government asserts a substantial interest, (3) the regulation directly advances that interest, and (4) the regulation is no more extensive than necessary to serve the government interest. 447 U.S. 557, 566. Critics have correctly suggested that *Central Hudson* did not allocate the burden of proof on the four parts, and failed to define what constituted sufficient proof to prevail on each. Wilcox, Shea, and Hovland, *Alcoholic Beverage Advertising and the Electronic Media,* 8:1 COM. & LAW 31, 36 (February 1986).

speech.[47] On the other hand, the Court found the necessary link in *Central Hudson,* concluding that there was "an immediate connection between advertising and demand for electricity" satisfying the required link between the ban on promotional ads and the state's interest in energy conservation.[48]

For a tobacco advertising ban to survive under the third prong of *Central Hudson,* proponents would have to demonstrate that eliminating tobacco ads would decrease consumption. Needless to say, this proposition is subject to considerable dispute among scholars. For instance, former FTC Chairman Michael Pertschuk, who favors a ban, argues that the countries that have reduced their percentage of smokers have only done so by banning tobacco advertising.[49] And some commentators have argued for the existence of a connection between advertising focused at women and the increased numbers of female smokers.[50] But overall, it is far from self-evident that an advertising ban would decrease consumption of tobacco.

To the contrary, critics have suggested multiple reasons why a tobacco advertising ban would not work. First, the 1971 ban on broadcast advertising was a failure. Cigarette smoking began to fall off during the period between 1967–1971 when the FCC required antismoking commercials. But, when the ban on broadcast ads went into effect in 1971, cigarette smoking increased, rather than decreasing even further. This was presumably because antismoking commercials, which had proven quite effective, were no longer being run. At any rate, since the ban on broadcast advertising failed to decrease tobacco consumption, critics are skeptical that a total advertising ban would be any more effective.

The second objection critics have raised is that banning all advertising will inevitably result in decreased costs to the tobacco companies, since unlike with the 1971 partial ban, there will be no opportunity to shift the $2.5 billion currently spent annually on advertising to other media. There is at least the theoretical possibility that a decrease in advertising costs will lead to lower prices and higher consumption.[51]

A third objection is based on the fact that the Synar bill does not make a content distinction between various types of advertising. This would mean, for instance, that factual advertising promoting the relative safety of a certain brand of low tar cigarette would be prohibited just as if it were an image advertisement showing a couple climbing a mountain while smoking high tar cigarettes.[52] There would therefore be no incentive to make low tar cigarettes, since the consuming public would not be aware the company was

---

47. 425 U.S. at 769.
48. 447 U.S. at 569.
49. Pertschuk, *Cigarette Ads and the Press,* Nation 283, 287 (March 7, 1987).
50. Garrison, *supra* note 10, at 203.
51. Colford, *Bill Curbs Unfairness Ad Power,* Ad. Age, March 16, 1987, at 70.
52. Although image advertising predominates now, as recently as 1979, 82 percent of all tobacco ads in magazines emphasized low tar and nicotine, according to one study. Rothenberg, *supra* note 27, at 6E, col. 1.

doing it.[53] To the extent that the Synar bill would result in a slower change to safer products, it would be counterproductive.

It is on this issue, the third prong of the *Central Hudson* test, that *Posadas* makes a profound change in the traditional first amendment analysis. Prior to *Posadas*, the Court had placed the burden on the government to prove that the speech restriction would directly advance a governmental interest. But in *Posadas* the Court found that it was enough that the Puerto Rican legislature "believed" that regulating speech, in this case casino advertising, would promote the specific governmental interest in the case, namely decreasing gambling by local citizens. The Court deferred to the legislative judgment without comment, suggesting that after *Posadas* the burden of proof has shifted, and now the advertiser has to prove that an advertising ban would not promote a legitimate government interest, instead of compelling the government to prove that it would.[54]

The importance of this change can be seen in the context of tobacco advertising, where there is no hard evidence one way or the other as to the efficacy of a ban, and the matter may come down to who has the burden of proof. Since the opponents of the ban now have the burden, it is doubtful that they could prevail on this issue. This is especially true since, after *Posadas*, it is sufficient if Congress simply "believes" that a tobacco advertising ban would work.

VI. WEIGHING ALTERNATIVES TO A BAN

The fourth and final prong of the *Central Hudson* test requires that any government attempt to restrict truthful commercial speech must be the most limited restriction available to the state. The least restrictive alternative prong of *Central Hudson* would provide the most difficult hurdle for the government to overcome in defending the Synar bill. The issue would be the existence of a feasible, less restrictive alternative to a complete ban on tobacco advertising, and it would seem that the government has at its disposal a number of alternatives.

As one example, the Court has expressed its preference for a policy of warnings and disclosures as a less restrictive alternative to bans on truthful

---

53. In the 1950s, cigarette firms competed to reduce tar and nicotine and actually lowered the content of each by 30 to 40 percent. Then in 1960, the FTC was the catalyst of an industry-wide ban on the advertising of tar and nicotine content. Because the consumer no longer received information on tar and nicotine content, it was no longer advantageous for tobacco companies to compete to reduce those substances, and they stopped. Subsequently, many public-service organizations decried the ban, the FTC changed its policy, and firms began again to compete with regard to tar and nicotine content, advertising their lower and lower rates. Scheibla, *Not Just Blowing Smoke,* Ad. Age, March 2, 1987, at 11.
54. Younger, *Alcoholic Beverage Advertising on the Airwaves,* 34 U.C.L.A. L. REV. 1139, 1169 (1987).

information.[55] Congress has implemented a system of warnings and disclosures in tobacco advertisements. One alternative to a blanket ban would be to strengthen the tone of the warnings and to couple this with reinstitution of the counteradvertising campaign that occurred when the fairness doctrine was applied to tobacco.

In addition to counteradvertising, warnings, and disclosures, nonspeech-related alternatives to the blanket ban exist. Taxes are one feasible way in which demand can be dampened. Eliminating the deductibility of promotional expenditures, now being considered by Congress, would still allow tobacco companies to advertise, but would make it more costly to continue with the current level of advertising. If tobacco companies chose to reduce the volume of advertising, this could result in a reduction in tobacco consumption. On the other hand, if the tobacco companies chose to continue the current level of advertising and pass their increased costs on to the consumer, prices would increase and consumption should decline.[56]

Another nonspeech-related alternative to a blanket ban on tobacco advertising would be to ban tobacco products themselves. Certain commentators have suggested quite seriously that since an advertising prohibition would implicate the first amendment interests of advertisers and consumers, but a complete ban on tobacco products would not reach any constitutionally protected conduct, a tobacco ban would be a less restrictive alternative.[57]

In any event, most commentators have concluded that less restrictive alternatives, in one form or another, do exist. For this reason, whether an advertising ban could survive the fourth prong of the traditional *Central Hudson* test is highly questionable.

Here again, as with the third prong of *Central Hudson*, the judicial landscape was changed considerably by *Posadas*. Prior to *Posadas,* the Court invalidated most attempts by the state to restrict truthful commercial speech. Even when the government asserted an interest in protecting the public from forms of advertising having the potential for deception, the Court required that the state demonstrate that disclosures or warnings would not be an effective alternative to a blanket ban.

In *Posadas,* however, the Court took a much more deferential approach. Puerto Rico, seeking to avoid the ills attributable to gambling, failed to demonstrate the ineffectiveness of alternatives to a casino advertising ban, or to demonstrate that a prior legislative attempt with a less restrictive scheme showed the need for the present ban. Given this, the casino advertising ban in *Posadas* should have failed the fourth prong of *Central Hudson*. But the

---

55. *Central Hudson,* 447 U.S. at 570–71.
56. A considerable number of informative articles have been written focusing exclusively on the economics of the tobacco marketplace. *See, e.g.,* Schneider, Klein & Murphy, *supra* note 9, at 577–78.
57. Television program, "Free Speech and Advertising—Who Draws the Line?" Produced by Inst. for Democratic Com., College of Com., Boston Univ., at 1, 19 (1987).

Court addressed only the possibility of a counteradvertising alternative to the ban, concluding that it was "up to the legislature to decide whether or not such a 'counterspeech' policy would be as effective."[58] Although the Court stated that it was applying the *Central Hudson* test, it was utilizing a relaxed standard. The Court relieved the state of its burden of demonstrating that alternative restrictions would be ineffective, abandoning the least restrictive alternative analysis of *Central Hudson* for a lower, "rational basis" standard of review.

Applying *Posadas* to the Synar bill, it would appear not to be fatal that less restrictive alternatives to a total tobacco advertising ban do exist. Even in light of these alternatives, a court could find that, as in *Posadas,* the legislature simply decided the alternatives would not be as effective as a total advertising ban.

VII. CONCLUSION

Tobacco advertising does not merit first amendment protection, since speech which does no more than propose a commercial transaction does not add to the information in the public domain. And if tobacco advertising, like all commercial speech, is not protected by the first amendment, the state is free to regulate, or not regulate, tobacco advertising as it sees fit. This is already the case with other nonprotected speech, like obscenity. Since it is nonprotected speech, the proper forum for those opposed to the regulation of tobacco advertising is the legislature, not the courts.

At the administrative level, it would be a mistake to attempt to control tobacco advertising through FTC regulation, or regulation by any other administrative agency, which labels tobacco advertising as *per se* misleading. Tobacco advertising is no more or less misleading than advertising for any other product. Moreover, these back-door attempts to ban tobacco advertising should give way to legislation like the Synar bill, which confronts the issue directly.

If legislation is going to be promulgated which bans the advertisement of lawful products, as was done in *Posadas,* it is most difficult to see how any meaningful first amendment distinction can be drawn between tobacco and any other product. The Court has to make an "all-or-nothing" decision, either denying all first amendment protection for commercial speech, as in *Valentine v. Chrestensen,* or extending broad first amendment protection to commercial speech, as in *Virginia Pharmacy.*

The *Posadas* approach, which finds that commercial speech is protected

58. 106 S. Ct. at 2978.

by the first amendment, but then reduces the actual protection to almost nothing, is highly unsatisfactory.

The Court should return to the theoretical underpinnings of the first amendment and announce, as it did the first time it ever considered the issue in 1942, that commercial speech is wholly outside the first amendment.[59]

59. Valentine v. Chrestensen, 316 U.S. 52 (1942).

Readings from COMMUNICATIONS AND THE LAW, 1

The articles collected in *Defamation: Libel and Slander* were published in the following issues of COMMUNICATIONS AND THE LAW.

"Herbert v. Lando: No Cause for Alarm," by Howard E. Goldfluss, originally appeared in vol. 1, no. 3, pp. 61-68, © 1979.

"Herbert v. Lando: Threat to the Press, Or Boomerang for Public Officials?" by Andre E. Briod, originally appeared in vol. 2, no. 2, pp. 59-92, © 1980.

"Fashioning a New Libel Defense: The Advent of Neutral Reportage," by Donna Lee Dickerson, originally appeared in vol. 3, no. 3, pp. 77-86, © 1981.

"The Future of Strict Liability in Libel," by F. Dennis Hale, originally appeared in vol. 5, no 2, pp. 23-37, © 1983.

"Protecting Confidential Sources in Libel Litigation," by Anthony Green, originally appeared in vol. 6, no. 3, pp. 39-51, © 1984.

"Retraction's Role Under the Actual Malice Rule," by Donna Lee Dickerson, originally appeared in vol. 6, no. 4, pp. 39-51, © 1984.

"Libel and the Long Reach of Out-of-State Courts," by Donna Lee Dickerson, originally appeared in vol. 7, no. 4, pp. 27-43, © 1985.

"Problems in Libel Litigation," by Erik L. Collins, Jay B. Wright and Charles W. Peterson, originally appeared in vol. 7, no. 5, pp. 41-57, © 1985.

"Avoiding the Chilling Effect: News Media Tort and First Amendment Insurance," by Robert L. Spellman, originally appeared in vol. 7, no. 6, pp. 13-27, © 1985.

"'Innocent Construction' Rule Survives Challenge," by Kyu Ho Youm and Harry W. Stonecipher, originally appeared in vol. 7, no. 6, pp. 43-60, © 1985.

"'Single Instance' Rule as a Libel Defense," by Kyu Ho Youm, originally appeared in vol. 9, no. 4, pp. 49-65, © 1987.

"Libel as Communication Phenomena," by Jeremy Cohen and Albert C. Gunther, originally appeared in vol. 9, no. 5, pp. 9-30, © 1987.

"Fact or Opinion: Where to Draw the Line," by Robert L. Spellman, originally appeared in vol. 9, no. 6, pp. 45-61, © 1987.

"Constitution Provides Limited Libel Protection to Broadcast Commentators," by Don Sneed, Whitney S. Mandel, and Harry W. Stonecipher, originally appeared in vol. 10, no. 2, pp. 19-30, © 1988.

Readings from COMMUNICATIONS AND THE LAW, 2

The articles collected in *Privacy and Publicity* were published in the following issues of COMMUNICATIONS AND THE LAW.

"The Public and the Fair Credit Reporting Act," by Blair C. Fensterstock, originally appeared in vol. 2, no. 1, pp. 31-43, © 1980.

"Resolving the Press-Privacy Conflict: Approaches to the Newsworthiness Defense," by Theodore L. Glasser, originally appeared in vol. 4, no. 2, pp. 23-42, © 1982.

"Motor Vehicle Records: Balancing Individual Privacy and the Public's Legitimate Need to Know," by Leslie G. Foschio, originally appeared in vol. 6, no. 1, pp. 15-20, © 1984.

"The Television Docudrama and the Right of Publicity," by Deborah Manson, originally appeared in vol. 7, no. 1, pp. 41-61, © 1985.

"The Big Dan's Rape Trial: An Embarrassment for First Amendment Advocates and the Courts," by Susanna R. Barber, originally appeared in vol. 7, no. 2, pp. 3-21, © 1985.

"The Freedom of Information Act Privacy Exemption: Who Does It Really Protect?," by Kimiera Maxwell and Roger Reinsch, originally appeared in vol. 7, no. 2, pp. 45-59, © 1985.

"Privacy Invasion Tort: Straddling the Fence," by Deckle McLean, originally appeared in vol. 7, no. 3, pp. 5-30, © 1985.

"Unauthorized Use of Deceased's Persona: Current Theories and the Need for Uniform Legislative Treatment," by Valerie B. Donovan, originally appeared in vol. 7, no. 3, pp. 31-63, © 1985.

"Press and Privacy Rights Could Be Compatible," by Deckle McLean, originally appeared in vol. 8, no. 2, pp. 13-25, © 1986.

"Photojournalism and the Infliction of Emotional Distress," by Michael D. Sherer, originally appeared in vol. 8, no. 2, pp. 27-37, © 1986.

"Recognizing the Reporter's Right to Trespass," by Deckle McLean, originally appeared in vol. 9, no. 5, pp. 31-42, © 1987.

"The 1978 Right to Financial Privacy Act and U.S. Banking Law," by Roy L. Moore, originally appeared in vol. 9, no. 6, pp. 23-44, © 1987.

"Unconscionability in Public Disclosure Privacy Cases," by Deckle McLean , originally appeared in vol. 10, no. 2, pp. 31-44, © 1988.

"Docudramas and False-Light Invasion of Privacy," by Tim A. Pilgrim originally appeared in vol. 10. no. 3, pp. 3-37, © 1988.

Readings from COMMUNICATIONS AND THE LAW, 3

The articles collected in *Censorship, Secrecy, Access, and Obscenity* were published in the following issues of COMMUNICATIONS AND THE LAW.

Readings from COMMUNICATIONS AND THE LAW, 4

The articles collected in *Advertising and Commercial Speech* were published in the following issues of COMMUNICATIONS AND THE LAW.